The Fish
Cookbook
Journal
and Tales

Minnetonka, Minnesota

About the Author

Author Robin Krause was born in western Kansas and was raised on her family's small farm. She received her undergraduate degree in Foods and Nutrition from Kansas State University. Robin moved to Minneapolis, Minnesota, to work for a major food company. She attended LaVarenne cooking school and developed a freelance food consultant and food styling business. At work and at home, Robin is a passionate cook and artist in the design and presentation of food. Robin relates her appreciation for food to her deep respect for the earth and the bountiful harvest it provides; all senses are touched by the goodness of the land and the waters. Robin connects with the soil through her garden, and enjoys fishing the rivers and lakes of the Midwest.

The Fish Cookbook Journal and Tales

By Robin Krause

Printed in 2011.

Tom Carpenter
Creative Director

Dan Kennedy
Book Production Manager

Michele Teigen
Book Development Coordinator

Zachary Marell
Designer

Phil Aarrestad
Photography

Special thanks to the Mullvain & Wright Families

6 7 8 / 15 14 13 12 11
© 1998 North American Fishing Club
ISBN 10: 1-58159-014-8
ISBN 13: 978-1-58159-014-2

North American Fishing Club
12301 Whitewater Drive
Minnetonka, MN 55343
www.fishingclub.com

Table of Contents

Introduction 4

The Fish and Its Ingredients 8

Bass 14

Catfish 30

Northern Pike 48

Panfish 56

Perch 74

Salmon 82

Steelhead 98

Trout 106

Walleye 120

Fish and Its Crusts 138

Relish, Salsa and Pesto 146

Index 156

We dedicate this cookbook to: the anglers who shared with us

their stories and their passion for fishing, as well as all the other

North American Fishing Club members who live to wet a line; to those

who are presently respecting the waters, their bounty and tradition;

and to those who will continue to preserve what has been passed

down for generations. The catch-and-release ethic is alive and well,

but now and again we all save a few "for the pan."

Cook over an open fire, gather a blend of spiced wood and briquettes or simply pan fry.

Share the passion...

Cooking, like fishing, is an adventure: a hobby, a passion and a skill that grows richer over time. The angler and the angler-cook both have perseverance, drive, inner as well as physical strength, endurance, focus, organization and talent. In both fishing and cooking, you can preserve and expand knowledge through sharing the passion with those who are also interested.

Carry it with you...

The Fish Cookbook Journal & Tales is a collection of recipes, stories and tales which will take you on a new adventure in the kitchen, the cabin or in the wilderness. Carry this journal with you to your favorite fishing hole. Cook over an open fire, gather a blend of spiced wood and briquettes or simply pan fry. Entire meals can be prepared in remote cabins, tents or on a boat deck ... and in your kitchen at home, of course!

Relish your catch...

This Journal contains 11 chapters: One on relishes, one on crusts, and one on each of the nine most common varieties of freshwater fish. The introduction to each fish chapter features a story sent to us from an NAFC member. Taken as a whole these stories reflect the myriad of personalities, fishing styles and motivations our sport encompasses. Individually the stories provide practical tips, observations, or simply one person's memorable experience fishing for that particular type of fish.

Cherish each season...

The "Prize Catch" recipes listed at the beginning of each chapter offer menus for Spring, Summer, Winter and Fall. These recipes urge you to take advantage of fresh produce during its harvest season.

Expand your knowledge...

Sprinkled among the recipes you will find little gems of information — tidbits of background, facts and tips on particular ingredients. Blending techniques with natural herbs and ingredients is similar to understanding nature's dynamics found in ponds, lakes and streams. Knowledge is wealth.

Enjoy!

Enjoy the wild and preserve the natural taste. Remember to preserve the habitat and only take what fish you need for a delicious meal or two. Savor those special meals, with recipes from this book. Have respect and graciously reflect on the game, and all of its bounty.

Sprinkled among the recipes you will find little gems of information — tidbits of background, facts and tips on particular ingredients.

Some anglers tend to favor pot cooking, where practically the whole meal is cooked in one pot to accommodate the outdoor lifestyle. They use fresh ingredients from farmer's markets, farms and gardens, and are attracted to the simpleness of life. They laugh heartily, they fish and eat with great enthusiasm. They are eager to share fish with friends or show them how to fillet a fish. They know what goes in their pantry and we've added to their list.

The Rustic Pantry

The Garlic Family

The garlic family includes its cousins—onions, leeks, shallots and chives. The leek and the shallot often impart a more delicate flavor than onion or garlic.

The Tacklebox Spices

These convenient spices include thyme, rosemary, sage, parsley, basil, Italian parsley, oregano, dill, fennel, bay leaf and (of course) salt and pepper.

Fresh and dried herbs add tremendous flavor to fish. The recipes in this book most often call for fresh herbs, but one-third the amount of dried may be substituted for fresh. Basil is always best fresh and should not be added to a dish until the dish is cooked. Recipes which call for dried herbs—the sauces, crusts or fish batters—work well with these herbs.

The Nightshade Family

Vine-ripened tomatoes are available all year round with the peak season from June through September. These tomatoes are succulent, fragrant and richly colored. Beefsteak, plum, cherry and pear tomatoes vary in acidity. Green tomatoes have a piquant flavor while

yellow and orange tomatoes are sweeter in taste. When fresh are not available use canned Italian-style plum tomatoes or prepare the recipes that call for ripe tomatoes when they are in season.

The Ancient Tuber

The Incas were cultivating the humble potato thousands of years ago. The four categories here are russet, long white, round white and round red. Keep these varieties along with sweet potatoes and some of the heirloom potatoes in a cool, dry, dark place.

Farmer's Market Vegetables

Here you have salad greens, spinach, corn on the cob, squash, asparagus, carrots, cucumbers and zucchini. Try to cook with these vegetables when they are in season. The flavor is better, the price is cheaper and it's a natural way to enjoy nature's bounty.

Canned Goods in the Grub Box

Canned tomatoes, chicken broth and beans are really the only canned goods you'll need.

Bottled Goods in the Grub Box

Olive oil, vinegar, mustard, Worcestershire sauce and olives are musts. Don't forget the wine and beer, for special accents and extra zing.

Bulk Staples in the Grub Box

Keep flour, sugar, cornmeal, dry beans, pasta, coffee and tea on hand. Blend your favorite crust mixtures from this book before taking off for your fishing outing. Pack them along to sprinkle on the catch, or to season vegetables.

Dairy for the Cooler

Butter, eggs, milk, cheese and cream for the coffee.

Blend your favorite crust mixtures from this book, and pack them along.

Fire &

Fire is as fascinating and mesmerizing as the hypnotic rhythm of a perfect cast. Fire's coziness, inspiration and passion directly translate to the food. Fish can be cooked on just about any kind of grill, from a cooking rack over a campfire to an elaborate gas grill.

The Angler-Cook's Tools: Fire and Smoke

► For cooking small fish and fillets, an open grill works best. For large whole fish, a covered grill is ideal; the hot air inside creates an oven, so the flesh cooks through before the skin chars.

► Anglers like to use an all-wood fire to bring out fish's best flavor, but charcoal briquettes work well too and are sometimes more convenient. Of course, a gas or electric grill can be used, but the flavor will not be quite as smoky or savory.

► For wood fires, make sure the wood you use is whole untreated hardwood, not softwood or any kind of processed wood, including lumber that might contain chemicals.

► Wood takes longer to reach the grilling stage of coal-readiness (about 1 hour), and has a higher ash content than charcoal.

► Using half hardwood charcoal and half wood is a good way to add the fragrance of wood smoke to your food. Wood smoke will lend a strong, smoky flavor to any grilled fish.

► For hardwood charcoal (mesquite, oak or ash), prepare a single layer of large chunks covering an area somewhat larger than you intend to grill over. For briquettes, spread a layer 2 briquettes deep. Start the fire with pine cones or dried grass; newspapers or electric starters are fine too. Don't use chemical starters or chemically-treated briquettes; they can alter the food's taste.

► Topping the coals with wood chips, especially mesquite or alder, will impart a pleasant woodsmoke flavor to the fish. Soak the chips in water for at least half an hour to keep them from burning too fast.

► After the fire is lit, wait at least half an hour for the flames to die down. Most fish cooks best over a hot to medium-hot fire. A seared, grid-marked exterior contrasts beautifully with the tender interior flesh.

- You're ready to grill when a white ash forms over the coals and the embers glow red. Spread the coals out a bit before cooking.

- Try adding sturdy herb branches like rosemary and bay when grilling. If you've got a flourishing herb garden, trim one or two branches from the herb plant, soak in water and throw on the fire. Grapevines or lemon branches (which don't need to be soaked) also add a nice aroma to the fire.

- The grill rack should be at least 5 inches from the coals. Allow the rack to get sufficiently hot so that the fish sears slightly and forms a firm exterior that holds in the juices and makes the fish easier to turn.

- Oil both the grill and the fish to prevent sticking. Try not to turn fish more than once; most are delicate and may fall apart.

- For the grill, you can control the heat and prevent flare-ups by using the grill vents; open vents create a hotter fire, closed or partially closed vents, a cooler one.

In this book, we recommend the natural fuel sources — hardwood charcoal and wood; they add smokiness, char and flavor to food. But you can still obtain good results with charcoal briquettes or a gas grill.

Grilling and Cooking Basics

Although we have tested and timed our recipes, our cooking times must be considered suggestions only, as so many variables affect how fast fish cooks on the grill or on an open fire. The temperature of the fish, the fire and the air are important factors, as is the level of humidity and wind conditions. On damp days, foods will cook more slowly; wind will make a fire burn hotter. Hardwood charcoal, including mesquite, burns hotter than briquettes.

We recommend that the fish grilled or cooked be at room temperature at the time it's put on the grill or fire. This temperature is very important to ensure good grilling, gives more control over the length of cooking time, and will allow any food to cook more evenly.

Two visual clues will tell you when a fish is done. The flesh of the fish will begin to separate into its natural segments, and it will turn from translucent to opaque. Through experience, you will learn to tell the doneness of fish by touch; like chicken breasts, fish are done when they are firm yet springy to the touch, not soft or stiff.

Most importantly, enjoy the calm of the day, the nature that surrounds and the warmth of the grill or fire.

Keep in mind the doneness guide developed by the Canadian Department of Fisheries: Cook any fish for 10 minutes per inch of thickness (measuring the fish at its thickest point). So a 1-inch-thick fillet or steak should be cooked for 5 minutes on each side, and a ¾-inch thick fillet or steak should be cooked for 3-4 minutes on each side.

Whole fish with the skin on may be cooked a little longer, as the skin helps to keep the fish moist and intact. Although there are many variables in grilling that may slightly alter this rule, it's amazing how accurate it usually is.

It is much easier to tell when fillets, steaks and cut pieces of fish are done than it is to determine the doneness of a whole fish. Large whole fish is done when an instant-read thermometer inserted into its thickest part and not touching the backbone reads 140°F. If you don't have a thermometer, cut into the fish and look for flakiness and opacity.

In the recipes, the size of the whole fish and fillets are only a guideline. There are wide ranges for the average sizes of fish. If your fish or fillets are larger than those recommended, adjust the cooking time appropriately.

Most importantly, enjoy the calm of the day, the nature that surrounds and the warmth of the grill or fire. Stay near the fire and keep an eye on the coals; adjust the rack if needed. Remember, undercooked fish can go back on the grill, but overcooked fish stays dry and overcooked.

General Notes on Cleaning, Handling and Filleting Fish

Anyone who has eaten his or her own catch knows that fish are best when cooked and eaten as fresh as possible, right off the hook.

Fresh Fish

For fish to be eaten soon after they are caught, de-gill and gut the fish. After thumbing out the kidneys and washing out the cavity, thoroughly dry it. Place the fish on ice or in a creel lined with dampened ferns.

If the fish are larger—salmon, steelhead or trophy-sized trout— bleed them by sticking them just behind the gill, then cover and tie them (air free) in a plastic tube. The tube should be cut off a roll with a length to accommodate the fish plus two knots. Lay the fish in the stream to keep cool.

If you are driving home with the fish and preparing the fish the next day, do not gut and gill the fish until you get home. Put the fish on ice. Pour or drain off the water as it accumulates, as water is a carrier of the bacteria that spoil flesh.

Freezing Fish

Fish kept on ice will remain reasonably flavorful for two days. Do not keep fish longer than four to eight hours in the refrigerator before freezing. All fish deteriorates in flavor after frozen, but you can reduce this deterioration markedly by freezing the fish in a block of ice or with a thin layer of ice over its surface.

Filleting Fish

In filleting fish, try to start the process by using a fillet knife that is as flexible as possible and has a narrow blade curving to a sharp point. It should also be razor sharp.

Lay the fish on a board; cut down to the spine and around the sides. Do not cut the spine in two. Cut into fish behind the transverse cut and slice toward the tail, cutting down to, but not through, the ribcage. When you have sliced down two-thirds of the length of the fish (where it begins to taper), push the point clear through, keeping the flat of the blade close along the backbone. Holding the fish with the left hand, continue to cut close against the backbone all the way to the tail. Now lay the fillet open and finish cutting the flesh away from the ribcage. Slice it loose along the belly line, turn the fish over, and duplicate process on the other side.

To remove skin, place the fillet on the board, skin side down, and take hold of the tip of the fillet with the left hand. Cut in between skin and flesh, then change your grip with the left hand. Hold tight onto the skin tip while you slice forward, pressing the flat of the knife blade down as you slice forward.

Anyone who has eaten his or her own catch knows that fish are best when cooked and eaten as fresh as possible, right off the hook.

Bass

The Leaping Bass

For the cook...

Besides being unmatched fighters on the appropriate bait, largemouth and small-mouth bass can compete with other game fish in flavor with their firm, white flesh. The lucky angler who decides to keep maybe a bass or two for dinner should fillet and skin the fish. With the firm, mild texture and flavor of bass, you can bake, grill, broil or fry. Bass is also delicious in soups and chowders.

For the angler...

Largemouths and smallmouths, with their jolting strikes and rambunctious leaps, are among the most exciting game fish. Freshwater bass are members of the sunfish family. Catching bass, as outlined in Mr. Kimball's letter, is not for those in a hurry. But, then again, if rushed, why fish?

For us all...

Fishing at its finest erases the past two hundred years of mankind's evolution. It propels us back in time to an era when our own rhythms more closely matched those of all other creatures. Modern technological culture, where efficiency is measured in nano-seconds, is made mockery of by those lovely, lingering moments between baiting and the bite.

All of us have suffered time after time when a bass would dart at our lure, only to keep a safe distance, rejecting anything and everything we offer. It is the kind of thing that will make you want to pack up and go home. Usually these bass are close to shore or in an area where they are highly visible. Don't give up. Try the fly rod instead. A medium-sized bream popper can liven up the day with a healthy catch. I prefer to use a white popper with a black and yellow feathered tail. Don't get in a hurry. Just drop the popper in the area where the bass rejected your offering and let it lay. After at least a minute-and-a-half to two minutes, give the popper the slightest twitch, barely moving it. You will find the bass is watching it carefully, and the slightest sign of life will cause him to act. He may wait for a while, but don't get in a hurry. Most of the time he will eventually strike. I have caught several bass well over 4 pounds with this technique. And, after all, a bass on a fly rod is a great experience. Try it. You'll be hooked in just a few tries.

Keith W. Kimball
Four Oaks, NC

Potatoes, corn and autumn orchard
apples flavor this fish chowder
that is easy to make over the campfire.

Fish, Corn
and Apple Chowder

8 slices bacon, cut into 1-inch pieces
4 bass fillets (about 1 pound)
8 ounce bottle clam juice
6 medium red potatoes, cut into ½-inch pieces
2 onions, chopped
2 tart apples, chopped
2 cups fresh corn kernels
2 teaspoons dried thyme leaves
1 teaspoon coarse ground pepper
1 pint half and half

Place bacon and fish in Dutch oven. Cook over medium heat, about 3 minutes per side. Remove fillets from pan; set aside. In same pan with bacon add remaining ingredients except half and half and sautéed fish. Continue cooking, stirring occasionally, for 15 to 20 minutes or until vegetables are tender. Stir in half and half, and sautéed fish. Cook over low heat for 8 to 10 minutes or until chowder is heated through.

4 servings.

*Lentils, carrots, tomatoes and fish simmer together in a curried broth
that is a comfort food on a cold winter's night.*

Fish and Lentil Soup

4 strips bacon, cut into ½-inch pieces
4 bass fillets (about 1 pound)
1 onion, sliced
2 carrots, sliced
2 stalks celery, sliced
2 cloves garlic, coarsely chopped
2 bay leaves
1 cup brown lentils
2 (14 ½-ounce) cans chicken broth
28-ounce can Italian-style tomatoes, cut up
1 tablespoon curry powder
1 teaspoon salt
½ teaspoon tumeric
½ teaspoon coarse ground pepper

Place bacon and fish in Dutch oven. Cook over medium heat, about 3 minutes
per side. Remove fillets from pan; set aside. In same pan with bacon, add onion,
carrots, celery and bay leaves. Cook, stirring occasionally, for 10 to 12 minutes
or until vegetables are browned. Stir in remaining ingredients except sautéed
fish. Bring mixture to a boil, reduce the heat and simmer, covered. Simmer for
25 to 30 minutes or until lentils are just tender. Stir in sautéed fish.

6 servings.

Onion, tomatoes, garlic and herbs
season a rich, broth stew that thickens while it cooks.

Summertime Tomato and Fish Stew

STEW

½ cup chopped fresh fennel weed
2 (14 ½-ounce) cans chicken broth
8-ounce bottle clam juice
6-ounce can tomato paste
8 ripe tomatoes, chopped
1 onion, chopped
1 bulb fennel, sliced, separated into rings
4 cloves garlic, coarsely chopped
2 bay leaves
½ teaspoon salt
½ teaspoon coarse ground pepper

BASS

6 bass fillets (about 1 ½ pounds)
2 tablespoons olive oil
2 tablespoons red wine vinegar
2 tablespoons chopped fresh basil leaves

Make the stew: place all broth ingredients into a large stockpot. Simmer, uncovered, about 1 hour. If desired, cover and chill. This can be made ahead and refrigerated up to 3 days.

Prepare the fish: place fillets in a large skillet with butter. Sauté fish over medium-high heat, about 3 minutes on each side. Sprinkle with vinegar and basil; add sautéed fillets to stew in stock pot. Simmer for 15 to 20 minutes or until heated through.

8 servings.

A fish broth soup with carrots, peas and fresh springtime bass is a light,
flavorful soup to serve with an egg salad sandwich.

Tender Spring Pea and Fish Soup

FISH BROTH
4 pounds bones and heads of bass
1 gallon water
1 medium onion, sliced
1 carrot, cut into pieces
1 leek, trimmed and washed, sliced
2 sprigs each, fresh thyme and parsley
1 bay leaf
½ teaspoon salt
2 cups white wine

SOUP
4 bass fillets (about 1 pound)
1 tablespoon butter
2 carrots, sliced
1 pound green peas, shelled
¼ teaspoon fresh ground pepper

Make the fish broth: place all broth ingredients, except wine into a large stockpot. Simmer, uncovered, about 30 minutes. Add wine; simmer 20 to 30 minutes.
Strain the liquid. Cover; refrigerate. Broth will keep 1 week in the refrigerator, or
about 4 months in the freezer.

Prepare the soup: place fillets in a large skillet with butter. Sauté fish over medium-high heat, about 3 minutes on each side. Simmer fish broth with carrots for
15 to 20 minutes or until carrots are tender. Add sautéed fish, peas and pepper.
Simmer for 5 to 6 minutes or until heated through.

6 servings.

Soak chunks of stale bread in vinegar, and then toss with tomatoes, onions, celery and basil-seasoned bass.

Bread and Tomato Salad

SALAD
1 loaf stale rustic country bread
4 ripe Roma tomatoes, seeded and chopped
½ cup chopped red onion
¼ cup sliced green onions
2 stalks celery, sliced
¼ cup torn fresh basil leaves
1 tablespoon chopped fresh oregano leaves
2 tablespoons olive oil
1 tablespoon balsamic vinegar
¼ teaspoon sugar
¼ teaspoon coarse salt
¼ teaspoon coarse ground pepper

BASS
2 teaspoons olive oil
3 bass fillets (about 1 pound)
1 tablespoon balsamic vinegar
½ teaspoon coarse ground pepper
2 tablespoons torn fresh basil leaves

Make the salad: cut the top off the loaf of bread and pull out all the bread inside, leaving the crust as a shell. Save the crust shell to feed the birds or use as bait. Sprinkle the bread pieces and the removed top crust with water and let stand for about 15 minutes, then squeeze out the moisture with a paper towel. Tear the bread into bite-sized pieces. Stir together the bread, tomatoes, red and green onions, celery, ¼ cup basil and oregano in medium bowl. Whisk together olive oil, vinegar, sugar, salt and pepper. Just before serving, pour the dressing over bread mixture; toss to combine.

Prepare the fish: heat olive oil in large skillet. Place fish in pan; sauté over medium-high heat, about 3 minutes on each side. Sprinkle with vinegar, pepper and basil leaves. Continue sautéing for 1 to 2 minutes or until fish flakes with fork. Flake fish into pieces; mix into salad.

4 servings.

Sauté crisp apples and bass fillets together in butter,
then top with browned butter walnuts.

Bass with Walnut Butter and Apples

¼ cup butter
4 bass (about 8 to 10 ounces each), cleaned, scaled
¼ teaspoon salt
¼ teaspoon pepper
2 tart apples, cored and sliced
1 sweet onion, thinly sliced
½ cup chopped walnuts
1 tablespoon chopped fresh sage leaves

Heat 2 tablespoons butter until sizzling in a large skillet. Place fillets in skillet; season with salt and pepper. Sauté over medium-high heat, about 4 minutes on each side or until firm to the touch and browned. Remove from pan; set aside. In same pan melt remaining 2 tablespoons butter; add apples, onions, walnuts and sage. Sauté, stirring occasionally, about 5 minutes or until apples and onions are tender and begin to brown. Garnish with sage leaves.

4 servings.

Blend thyme, parsley and sage leaves with Parmesan cheese for the crust of pan-fried bass fillets.

Herb Crusted Bass

1 cup grated fresh Parmesan cheese
¼ cup finely chopped fresh parsley
2 teaspoons finely chopped fresh thyme leaves
2 teaspoons finely chopped fresh sage leaves
4 bass fillets (about 1 ¼ pounds)
2 tablespoons butter

Combine Parmesan cheese, parsley, thyme and sage. Coat both sides of bass fillets with crumb mixture. Melt butter in large skillet until sizzling. Sauté fish about 4 minutes on each side or until fish flakes with fork.

4 servings.

Grill bass with a cornmeal, flour and sesame coating.

Lemon Sesame Bass

1 cup flour
1 cup stone ground cornmeal
½ cup toasted sesame seeds
1 tablespoon dried thyme leaves
1 teaspoon coarse salt
1 teaspoon coarse ground pepper
2 (about 2 pounds each) whole bass, cleaned
1 egg, slightly beaten
Juice of 1 lemon

Prepare grill or wood fire: heat until coals are ash white or a fire has burned down to coals. Combine flour, cornmeal, sesame seeds, thyme, salt and pepper. Clean, wash and pat dry fish. Dip fish in egg. Coat both sides of fish with flour mixture. Place on oiled grill rack; squeeze lemon on each fish. Grill over medium-hot coals about 10 minutes on each side or until fish flakes with fork.

6 servings.

Layer potato and onion slices to form the crust for this fish pie. Bass and red pepper is the filling. Top with fresh bread crumbs and Parmesan cheese that bakes to a crisp texture.

Potato, Onion and Fish Pie

5 tablespoons butter, melted
6 medium red potatoes, thinly sliced
2 sweet onions, thinly sliced
2 roasted red peppers, cut into 1-inch strips
3 bass fillets (about 1 pound), cut into strips
Juice of 1 lemon
2 cups plain low-fat yogurt
2 tablespoons curry powder
1 teaspoon salt
1 teaspoon coarse ground pepper
1 cup fresh bread crumbs, dried
3/4 cup grated fresh Parmesan cheese
1/4 cup stone ground cornmeal
1 tablespoon finely chopped fresh basil leaves
1 tablespoon finely chopped fresh parsley

Pour 3 tablespoons melted butter into glass 13 x 9-inch baking dish. Layer half of potatoes, onions, peppers and fish. Squeeze half of lemon juice over mixture. Layer half of yogurt, sprinkle with half of curry, salt and pepper. Repeat with remaining potatoes, onions, peppers and fish. Mix bread crumbs, cheese and cornmeal together in small bowl. Sprinkle crumb mixture over fish. Drizzle with remaining 2 tablespoons butter. Bake, covered at 375°F for 40 to 45 minutes. Remove foil. Continue to bake for 15 minutes or until browned. Sprinkle with fresh herbs.

6 servings.

Cut bass into pieces and pan-sear with corn.
Toss the bass and corn in a salad with tomatoes, cilantro and red onion.

Sweet Corn Salad

3 tablespoons olive oil
2 (about 10 ounces each) bass fillets
2 garlic cloves, coarsely chopped
2 anchovy fillets, minced
4 cups fresh corn kernels
1 tablespoon Dijon-style mustard
3 ripe tomatoes, chopped
3 tablespoons chopped fresh basil leaves
1 tablespoon chopped fresh cilantro leaves
1 red onion, thinly sliced
¼ cup sliced green onion
1 teaspoon coarse salt
½ teaspoon coarse ground pepper
2 tablespoons balsamic vinegar

Heat 1 tablespoon oil in large skillet over medium-high heat. Place fillets in skillet; sauté, about 4 minutes on each side. Remove from pan; flake into pieces. In same pan add remaining 2 tablespoons oil, garlic and minced anchovy. Cook, stirring occasionally, about 2 minutes or until they are lightly toasted. Add corn and mustard; continue cooking, stirring constantly, for about 4 minutes or until corn is roasted. In large bowl toss together roasted corn mixture, sautéed fish and remaining ingredients.

6 servings.

*Sauté bass, new potatoes, peppers and onions with tomatoes.
This hash is delicious with fried eggs.*

Campers' Fish Hash

3 tablespoons butter
8 medium red potatoes, thinly sliced
2 red peppers, chopped
1 red onion, chopped
3 cloves garlic, coarsely chopped
3 bass fillets (about 1 pound), cut into 1-inch pieces
2 ripe tomatoes, coarsely chopped
½ teaspoon coarse salt
½ teaspoon coarse ground pepper
1 tablespoon balsamic vinegar
2 tablespoons mixture of chopped fresh parsley and thyme leaves

Melt butter in large skillet until sizzling. Add potatoes; sauté over medium-high heat, turning occasionally, about 7 minutes or until potatoes start to brown. Add the peppers, onion and garlic. Continue to sauté, stirring occasionally, about 5 minutes or until vegetables are tender. Add the fish; sauté about 5 minutes or until fish flakes with fork. Add tomatoes, salt, pepper and vinegar. Stir in herbs.

To dine, prepare fried or poached eggs. Serve hash with eggs.

6 servings.

Bake garlic bass in foil with zucchini and carrots.

Garlic Roasted Bass

4 bass fillets (about 1 ½ pounds)
½ teaspoon coarse ground pepper
¼ teaspoon salt
2 roasted garlic bulbs
2 carrots, grated
2 zucchini, grated
2 tablespoons olive oil
¼ cup dry white wine

Heat oven to 400°F. Cut four 1-foot-square sheets of aluminum foil. Place a fillet on each sheet of foil. Season with pepper and salt. Divide roasted garlic, carrots and zucchini equally over each portion. Drizzle with olive oil and 1 tablespoon wine. Fold the aluminum foil to cover the fish. Bake the fish about 12 minutes or until fish flakes with fork.

To dine, place fish and vegetables on individual plates; pour juices over fish.

4 servings.

The Challenging Catfish

For the cook...

Many a boyhood story has been told about a bamboo pole, a can of worms, a "coal-oil" lantern and the quest for a great catfish. Many of these stories are shared over a campfire fish fry. Catfish is superb blackened, baked, grilled, broiled or sautéed. You can also pan-fry it in oil or sauté catfish in butter with a cornmeal crust. Keep the small catfish whole, and fillet the larger catfish.

For the angler...

The catfish is one of the fightin'est fish in the river. For those who dismiss them as "trash fish" suited only to foul waters, it must not be forgotten that members of this family swim side by side with walleye, pike, bass and sunfish in many streams. Catfish may be difficult for the novice to clean, but after a little practice they skin easily. Landing a huge catfish, as Mr. Jones' story illustrates, requires something beyond mere skill. In fact, landing any extraordinary fish calls for a little something extra.

For all of us...

Whatever amount of perseverance, patience, skill and experience we bring to the sport of fishing, the single factor we can't control is the fleeting, fickle blessing of luck. Then when we least expect it the hand of fortune, with a seemingly careless gesture, touches our humble efforts.

On a winter's night, I was sauger fishing on the Tennessee River in Morgan County, Alabama. The bite was slow and after four or five hours of fishing I had only four fish in the boat. I decided to take a break, pulled up on a drop-off and anchored down. My plan was to just throw out a couple of jigs tipped with minnows on the bottom. My first jig barely set down when I had to grab my rod and set the hook. It was 30 to 40 minutes later when I finally saw the fish for the first time. From the fight he put up, I imagined he was big, but once I caught a glimpse of him I was even more impressed.

It was a blue catfish that weighed in at 63 lb. 8 oz. This catch beat the world record for eight-pound-test line by a full five pounds !

The fish is now listed in the National Fresh Water Fishing Hall of Fame. Needless to say, I was amazed as anyone by my luck and know the Great Angler in the Sky was holding my line together.

Byron Jones
Morgan County, AL

The autumn gathering of nuts and seeds finds this recipe
being prepared with pecans, thyme and cream.

Blackened Catfish with Pecans

¼ cup sweet paprika
2 teaspoons cayenne pepper
1 teaspoon dried oregano leaves
1 teaspoon dried thyme leaves
½ teaspoon salt
½ teaspoon coarse ground pepper
6 (about 8-10 ounces each) catfish fillets
¼ cup melted butter
1 cup toasted pecans, coarsely chopped
½ cup heavy cream

Combine paprika, cayenne, oregano, thyme, salt and pepper in pie pan. Dip catfish in melted butter; coat with spice mixture. Heat a large cast-iron skillet over high heat until it is beyond the smoking stage and you see white ash in the skillet bottom, at least 10 minutes. Place fillets in hot pan; carefully spoon about 1 teaspoon melted butter on top of each fillet. Be careful, as the butter may flame up. Blacken, about 3 minutes until underneath is charred. Turn fish; spoon about 1 teaspoon melted butter on each fillet. Blacken, about 3 minutes or until fish flakes with fork. The time will vary according to the thickness of the fillet and the heat of the skillet. Repeat with remaining fillets. Remove fillets from pan; keep warm. Add toasted pecans to skillet; stir in cream. Cook over low heat for 4 to 5 minutes or until sauce is heated through.

To dine, serve cream sauce over fish.

6 servings.

The rub for this recipe is a mix of paprika, cayenne, pepper,
oregano and thyme. Sauté the catfish and the onions in butter,
then garnish with chives and fried spinach greens.

Blackened Catfish
with Fried Spring Onions

1 tablespoon sweet paprika

1 teaspoon salt

1 teaspoon cayenne pepper

1 teaspoon dried thyme leaves

1 teaspoon dried oregano leaves

1 teaspoon coarse ground pepper

6 (about 8-10 ounces each) catfish fillets

¼ cup melted butter

2 cups mixture of green onions, sweet onions, chives, sliced

3 cloves garlic, coarsely chopped

2 cups fresh spinach leaves, torn

Combine paprika, salt, cayenne, thyme, oregano and pepper in pie pan. Dip cat-fish fillets in melted butter; coat with spice mixture. Heat a large cast-iron skillet over high heat until it is beyond the smoking stage and you see white ash in the skillet bottom, at least 10 minutes. Place fillets in hot pan; carefully spoon about 1 teaspoon melted butter on top of each fillet. Be careful, as the butter may flame up. Blacken, about 3 minutes until underneath is charred. Turn fish; spoon about 1 teaspoon melted butter on each fillet. Blacken, about 3 minutes or until fish flakes with fork. The time will vary according to the thickness of the fillet and the heat of the skillet. Repeat with remaining fillets. Remove from heat, keep warm. Add onions and garlic to pan, sauté over medium heat about 5 min-utes or until somewhat blackened. Spoon onions over fish. Fry spinach over high heat about 3 minutes.

To dine serve fish with onions and garnish with spinach.

6 servings.

Ground mustard seeds and the cajun blackened spice
blend to make this catfish dinner
perfect for a winter night in the cabin.

Mustard Blackened Catfish

1 teaspoon yellow mustard seed, crushed
1 teaspoon brown mustard seed, crushed
1 teaspoon ground mustard
1 teaspoon dried thyme leaves
½ teaspoon salt
¼ teaspoon coarse ground pepper
6 (about 8-10 ounces each) catfish fillets
¼ cup melted butter
1 tablespoon red wine vinegar
2 tablespoons chopped fresh parsley

Combine the mustards, thyme, salt and pepper in pie pan. Dip catfish fillets in melted butter; coat with spice mixture. Heat a large cast-iron skillet over high heat until it is beyond the smoking stage and you see white ash in the skillet bottom, at least 10 minutes. Place fillets in hot pan; carefully spoon about 1 teaspoon melted butter on each fillet. Blacken, about 3 minutes until underneath is charred. Turn fish; spoon about 1 teaspoon melted butter on each fillet. Blacken, about 3 minutes or until fish flakes with fork. The time will vary according to the thickness of the fillet and the heat of the skillet. Repeat with remaining fillets. Remove from heat, keep warm.

To dine, sprinkle with vinegar and chopped parsley.

6 servings.

Blend a mixture of chili powder and other spices for the crust of the fish.
Salsa made from ears of summer corn and tomatoes create the relish.

Chile Blackened Catfish

CORN SALSA

2 cups fresh corn kernels

1 tablespoon olive oil

1 Anaheim chile pepper,
seeded, chopped

1 jalapeño chile pepper,
seeded, chopped

4 ripe tomatoes, chopped

1 tablespoon balsamic vinegar

2 tablespoons chopped
fresh cilantro

CATFISH

¼ cup chili powder

2 tablespoons cumin powder

2 teaspoons dried oregano leaves

1 teaspoon coarsely
ground pepper

½ teaspoon salt

6 (about 8-10 ounces each)
catfish fillets

¼ cup melted butter

Make the corn salsa: place corn in skillet with 1 tablespoon olive oil. Roast over medium heat, stirring occasionally, about 6 minutes or until tender. Add chile peppers; continue to sauté for 4 to 5 minutes or until corn begins to roast. Combine tomatoes, vinegar and cilantro with roasted corn and chile peppers. Cover and refrigerate. Salsa can be refrigerated up to 3 to 5 days.

Prepare the fish: combine chili powder, cumin, oregano, pepper and salt. Dip catfish in melted butter; coat with spice mixture. Heat a large cast-iron skillet over high heat until it is beyond the smoking stage and you see white ash in the skillet bottom, at least 10 minutes. Place fillets in hot pan; carefully spoon about 1 teaspoon melted butter on top of each fillet. Be careful, as the butter may flame up. Blacken, about 3 minutes until underneath is charred. Turn fish; spoon about 1 teaspoon melted butter on each fillet. Blacken, about 3 minutes or until fish flakes with fork. The time will vary according to the thickness of the fillet and the heat of the skillet. Repeat with remaining fillets.

To dine, present fish on corn salsa and garnish with sprig of cilantro.

6 servings.

Blacken peppers, onions and catfish. Serve with flour or corn tortillas.

Catfish Fajitas

1 teaspoon grated lime peel
¼ cup lime juice
2 tablespoons olive oil
1 teaspoon ground cumin
½ teaspoon coarse ground pepper
¼ teaspoon salt
⅛ teaspoon cayenne pepper
4 (about 8-10 ounces each) catfish fillets
2 onions, cut into wedges
2 red peppers
1 poblano or pasilla chile pepper
2 jalapeño or serrano chile peppers
8 flour or corn tortillas
Guacamole
Sour cream

Prepare grill or wood fire: heat until coals are ash white or a wood fire has burned down to coals. Meanwhile, stir together lime peel, lime juice, olive oil, cumin, pepper, salt and cayenne pepper in small bowl. Place catfish in plastic food bag. Pour in marinade; seal tightly. Place in 13 x 9-inch pan; let stand 10 to 15 minutes. Remove catfish from marinade; place on oiled grate of grill. Place onions and peppers around catfish. Grill catfish over medium-hot coals about 5 minutes on each side or until fish flakes with fork. Grill peppers about 6 minutes on each side or until charred. Place peppers in brown paper bag for 5 minutes to remove blackened skin. Cut peppers in half; remove seeds. Cut into strips. Grill tortillas about 2 minutes or until lightly toasted.

To dine, place onions and strips of peppers in bowl. Serve fish on grilled tortillas. Each person can make their own fajita by topping the fish with onions and peppers, guacamole and sour cream. Serve with lime wedges.

6 servings.

Catfish and red beans bake in the oven while the angler is on the lake or stream.

Catfish with Red Beans and Rice

BEANS AND RICE
2 cups red beans
1 sweet onion, thinly sliced
3 cloves garlic, coarsely chopped
½ teaspoon salt
½ teaspoon pepper
2 cups converted white or brown rice
2 teaspoons chopped fresh thyme leaves

CATFISH
2 tablespoons chile infused oil
6 (about 8-10 ounces each) catfish fillets
1 sweet onion, coarsely chopped
2 ripe tomatoes, coarsely chopped
2 teaspoons chopped fresh thyme leaves
¼ teaspoon cayenne pepper

Prepare the beans and rice: prepare the red beans according to package directions; add the onion, garlic, salt and pepper. Meanwhile prepare the rice according to package directions; add the thyme leaves.

Make the catfish: heat 1 tablespoon oil in large skillet; place 3 fillets in pan with half of the onion. Sauté over medium-high heat, about 3 minutes on each side. Repeat with remaining fillets and onion. Place all fillets in pan; add tomatoes, thyme and pepper. Sauté, stirring occasionally, for 2 to 3 minutes or until fish flakes with fork.

To dine, present fish on bed of rice and beans. Sprinkle with cayenne pepper.

6 servings.

Tomatoes, a handful of basil and cream
simmer together for a simple supper.

Catfish with Tomato Basil Cream

2 tablespoons butter
4 (about 8-10 ounces each) catfish fillets
4 cloves garlic, coarsely chopped
2 ripe tomatoes, coarsely chopped
¼ teaspoon salt
¼ teaspoon pepper
½ cup heavy cream
¼ cup torn fresh basil leaves

Heat butter until sizzling in large skillet. Place catfish in skillet; sprinkle with garlic. Sauté over medium-high heat, about 4 minutes on each side. Add tomatoes; season with salt and pepper. Continue cooking, about 2 minutes or until fish flakes with fork. Stir in cream; cook, stirring occasionally, about 2 minutes or until sauce is heated through. Stir in basil leaves.

To dine, slice additional tomatoes and place on individual serving plates. Place catfish on tomato slices; spoon sauce over fish.

4 servings.

Lemon, parsley and garlic
season cornmeal-coated catfish fillets.

Pan-Fried Catfish
with Lemon and Garlic

½ cup stone ground cornmeal
¼ cup flour
¼ cup finely chopped fresh parsley
2 teaspoons grated lemon peel
2 cloves garlic, finely chopped
4 (about 8-10 ounces each) catfish fillets
1 egg, slightly beaten
4 tablespoons butter
Juice of 1 lemon

Combine cornmeal, flour, parsley, lemon peel and garlic. Dip catfish fillets in
egg; coat with cornmeal mixture. Melt 2 tablespoons butter in large skillet until
sizzling. Place 2 catfish in skillet; cook over medium-high heat, about 4 minutes
on each side or until fish flakes with fork. Remove from pan; keep warm. Repeat
with remaining catfish. Sprinkle catfish with lemon juice.

4 servings.

Grill catfish with peppers, zucchini and onions. Serve this assortment
at room temperature with artichokes and olives.

Catfish Antipasto

4 (about 8-10 ounces each) catfish fillets
6 ounce jar marinated artichokes, reserve marinade
2 red peppers
2 medium zucchini or yellow squash
1 medium onion, cut into wedges
2 teaspoons chopped fresh rosemary leaves
½ teaspoon salt
½ teaspoon coarse ground pepper
12 kalamata olives
12 cherry tomatoes

Prepare grill or wood fire: heat until coals are ash white or a wood fire has
burned down to coals. Brush fillets with marinade from artichokes; place on
oiled grate of grill. Place peppers, zucchini and onion around fillets. Brush vegetables with remaining marinade. Season with rosemary, salt and pepper. Grill
over medium-hot coals, about 5 minutes on each side or until fish flakes with a
fork.

To dine, serve at room temperature with marinated artichokes, olives and cherry
tomatoes on bed of salad greens.

6 servings.

Spinach provides the bed for a casserole layered with sweet onions and catfish fillets.

Layered Spinach and Catfish Bake

1 tablespoon olive oil
2 sweet onions, thinly sliced
2 cloves garlic, coarsely chopped
4 cups torn fresh spinach leaves
2 tablespoons mayonnaise
2 teaspoons red pepper flakes
½ teaspoon salt
½ teaspoon coarse ground pepper
4 (about 8-10 ounces each) catfish fillets
2 teaspoons grated orange peel
Juice of 1 orange
2 tablespoons chopped fresh mint leaves

Heat olive oil in skillet; add onions and garlic. Sauté over medium heat, stirring occasionally, about 7 minutes or until browned. Gradually add spinach leaves; continue sautéing about 3 minutes or until spinach is wilted. Stir in mayonnaise, red pepper flakes, salt and pepper. Place in bottom of 13 x 9-inch baking dish. Layer catfish fillets on spinach mixture; sprinkle with orange peel and juice of orange. Bake at 375°F for 15 to 20 minutes or until fish flakes with fork. Sprinkle with mint leaves.

4 servings.

Buttermilk, mustard and cayenne pepper tenderize catfish fillets
dredged in seasoned bread crumbs, and deep-fat-fried.

Batter-Fried Catfish

1 cup fine dry bread crumbs

1 teaspoon dry mustard

1 teaspoon dried thyme leaves

½ teaspoon salt

½ teaspoon pepper

¼ teaspoon cayenne pepper

4 (8-10 ounces each) catfish fillets, cut into strips

1 cup buttermilk

1 quart vegetable oil

Combine bread crumbs, mustard, thyme, salt, pepper and cayenne pepper. Soak catfish fillets in buttermilk for 10 minutes; coat with bread crumb mixture. Place vegetable oil in a deep-fryer, wok or Dutch oven. Fry catfish fillets in hot oil about 2 to 3 minutes or until catfish is golden brown.

4 servings.

Cook okra gumbo in a skillet with pieces of catfish.

Fish and Okra Gumbo

2 pounds small okra
¼ cup vegetable oil
28 ounce can Italian-style plum tomatoes
1 onion, chopped
4 stalks celery, sliced
1 teaspoon salt
½ teaspoon cayenne pepper
4 bay leaves
½ teaspoon dried thyme leaves
2 quarts water
2 pounds catfish fillets, cut into pieces

Wash okra in cool water. Remove the caps and tips; cut into ¼-inch slices. Heat oil in large pot over medium-high heat. Fry the okra, stirring constantly, for 10 to 12 minutes or until most of the thick liquid of okra disappears. Add tomatoes, onions and celery. Cook, stirring often, for 15 minutes or until thick liquid has completely disappeared. Add remaining ingredients except catfish. Bring to a boil. Reduce the heat to medium; simmer for 15 minutes. Add catfish pieces. Continue to cook, stirring occasionally, for 20 minutes or until fish flakes with fork.

To dine, remove bay leaves and serve in deep bowls.

6 servings.

*Jambalaya is a spicy rice flavored with tomatoes
and accented with onions, garlic, spices and herbs.*

Catfish Jambalaya

2 tablespoons vegetable oil
2 onions, chopped
1 green pepper, chopped
4 stalks celery, sliced
2 pounds catfish fillets, cut into 1-inch pieces
4 bay leaves
14 ½-ounce can whole tomatoes, chopped, with juice
4 cloves garlic, coarsely chopped
1 teaspoon salt
½ teaspoon cayenne pepper
½ teaspoon coarse ground pepper
½ teaspoon dried thyme leaves
1 cup long grain white rice
¼ cup sliced green onions

Heat oil in large cast-iron Dutch oven over medium heat. Add onions, green pepper and celery; sauté for 7 to 8 minutes or until tender. Add catfish and bay leaves; sauté about 4 minutes or until catfish is browned. Add remaining ingredients except rice and onions. Cook for about 10 minutes, stirring often. Stir in rice. Cover; cook for 25 to 30 minutes or until rice is tender and liquid has been absorbed. Remove bay leaves; stir in green onions.

6 servings.

The Great Northern Pike

For the cook...

Swimming in clear weedy lakes, quiet pools and backwaters of creeks and rivers, we find the slender, spotted predator known as the northern pike. Because this sportfish is somewhat bony, the meat is drier than other fresh water fish. Basting and braising the fish with beer, wine or butter are the secret to adding moistness. Stuffing this fish adds flavor, and pan-roasting or grilling allows for an easy way to continue basting the fish while cooking.

For the angler...

As reflected in Mr. Walker's story, here, there are mysteries in fishing. These sweet mysteries are not to be solved, but only enjoyed. Fishing is a gamble: come with no expectations and you'll leave with a smile. Over time, most anglers, like Mr. Walker, come to appreciate the element of surprise in fishing.

For us all...

Like the seasoned gambler placing a bet before the cards are dealt, the wise angler surrenders expectation before the line is lowered. The pay-off of a winning hand hooks us on the sport.

I live in the small town of Wapakoneta in Northwestern Ohio. The small Augulaize River runs by my house. This swift, shallow river has a rocky bottom that is great for smallmouth bass, which I catch and release on a regular basis. The average bass is only a pound or so, so I use an ultra-lite rod with light line and a small crawdad crankbait.

One morning I was fishing when suddenly it felt as if I had snagged something. I figured it was carp. Suddenly the fish made a frantic zigzag and peeled off about 25 yards of line. I finally got the fish up to the bank and there was a 31-inch, 10-pound northern pike. I actually jumped in the water and threw the fish up on the bank!

Further investigation at the local library revealed that 75 years ago pike were native to the river. Most likely someone was fishing with minnows and had a pike minnow in their bucket and that is how he got there now.

Anyway, he is now hanging in my den and I am reminded of how lucky I am to have this nice little river nearby. I'm sure that those little smallies are resting just a little easier now, too.

Robert Walker
Wapakoneta, OH

Summer tomatoes are mixed
with garlic, capers and herbs to use
as the stuffing for northern pike.
Baste the fish with wine as it bakes.

Savory Tomato Stuffed Pike

1 tablespoon olive oil
2 ripe tomatoes, chopped
1 medium onion, chopped
1/3 cup capers
4 cloves garlic, coarsely chopped
1/2 cup mixture of chopped fresh herbs, Italian parsley, basil and oregano
2 northern pike (about 18 inches), cleaned, scaled with head removed
1/2 teaspoon salt
1/2 teaspoon coarse ground pepper
1/2 cup chopped fresh basil leaves
1/2 cup dry white wine

Heat olive oil in skillet; add tomatoes, onion, capers and garlic. Sauté over medium heat, stirring occasionally, about 5 minutes or until onion is tender. Stir in mixture of herbs. Stuff each of the northern pike with 1 cup tomato mixture. Place in broiler pan or large pan with sides. Sprinkle with salt and pepper. Bake at 375°F for 10 minutes. Pour wine over fish. Continue baking, basting every 10 minutes, for 20 minutes or until fish flakes with fork. Sprinkle with basil.

To bake, tie fish with kitchen string to enclose cavity and hold tomato mixture. Sprinkle any additional tomato mixture over fish.

6 servings.

Stuff dressed and scaled pike with onion, lemon
and the springtime watercress which grows along the creeks.
Wrap this stuffed fish in bacon to bake.

Onion Relish Stuffed Northern Pike

1 tablespoon olive oil
2 sweet onions, chopped
2 lemons, thinly sliced
4 cloves garlic, coarsely chopped
1 cup chopped watercress
2 northern pike (about 18 inches), cleaned, scaled with head removed
8 slices bacon
½ teaspoon salt
½ teaspoon coarse ground pepper
½ cup chopped fresh parsley

Heat olive oil in skillet; add onions, lemons and garlic. Sauté over medium heat, stirring occasionally, about 12 minutes or until caramelized. Stir in watercress. Stuff each of the northern pike with 1 cup onion mixture. Wrap each with 4 slices bacon; secure with wooden pick. Place in broiler pan or large pan with sides. Sprinkle with salt and pepper. Bake at 375°F, basting every 10 minutes for 30 minutes or until fish flakes with fork. Sprinkle with parsley.

To bake, tie fish with kitchen string to enclose cavity and hold onion mixture. Sprinkle any additional onion mixture over fish.

6 servings.

Tuck sugar and ginger glazed cranberries inside a northern pike.
Butter bastes the fish until it is golden brown. The cranberries
and a sprinkling of toasted nuts adds autumn's touch.

Fish with Glazed Cranberries

1 cup hazelnuts
1 cup pistachios
4 cloves garlic, coarsely chopped
1 tablespoon chopped fresh rosemary leaves
2 cups fresh or frozen cranberries
2 northern pike (about 18 inches), cleaned, scaled with head removed
½ teaspoon salt
½ teaspoon coarse ground pepper
½ cup dry white wine
Rosemary sprigs

Toast hazelnuts and pistachios in skillet or oven for 10 minutes. Remove skin
from hazelnuts. Coarsely chop toasted nuts. Stir together nuts, garlic, rosemary
and cranberries. Stuff each of the northern pike with 1 cup cranberry mixture.
Place in broiler pan or large pan with sides. Sprinkle with salt and pepper. Bake
at 375°F for 10 minutes. Pour wine over fish. Continue baking, basting every 10
minutes, for 20 minutes or until fish flakes with fork. Sprinkle with rosemary
sprigs.

To bake, tie fish with kitchen string to enclose cavity and hold cranberry mixture. Sprinkle any additional cranberry mixture over fish.

6 servings.

*Apple wedges from the orchard are sautéed in an
autumny brew. Use apple cider, beer or brandy
as the basting liquid while the whole fish bakes.*

Apple Sage Stuffed Northern Pike

2 tablespoons butter
2 tart apples, cored, sliced
1 sweet onion, chopped
1 tablespoon chopped fresh sage leaves
1 tablespoon hard cider or brandy
2 northern pike (about 18 inches), cleaned, scaled with head removed
½ teaspoon salt
½ teaspoon coarse ground pepper
⅓ cup hard cider or brandy
1 tablespoon grated orange peel
Sage leaves

Heat butter in skillet; add apples, onion and sage. Sauté over medium heat, stirring occasionally, about 8 minutes or until apples and onion are browned. Stir in sage and 1 tablespoon cider or brandy. Stuff each of the northern pike with about 1 cup apple mixture. Place in broiler pan or large pan with sides. Sprinkle with salt and pepper. Bake at 375°F for 10 minutes. Pour cider or brandy over fish. Continue baking, basting every 10 minutes, for 20 minutes or until fish flakes with fork. Sprinkle with orange peel and sage leaves.

To bake, tie fish with kitchen string to enclose cavity and hold apple mixture. Sprinkle any additional apple mixture over fish.

6 servings.

Season pike with Hungarian paprika and
smother the fish in sour cream. Red onion rings
and a sprinkling of parsley is the garnish.

Baked Pike
in Sour Cream and Paprika

1 cup sour cream
2 tablespoons mayonnaise
2 tablespoons sweet paprika
½ teaspoon salt
½ teaspoon coarse ground pepper
2 tablespoons chopped fresh parsley
2 northern pike (about 18 inches), cleaned, scaled with head and tail removed
2 medium red onions, sliced
¼ cup chopped fresh parsley

Stir together sour cream, mayonnaise, paprika, salt, pepper and 2 tablespoons
parsley in small bowl. Place fish in broiler pan or large pan with sides. Spread
sour cream mixture over fish; top with onion slices. Bake at 350°F for 25 to 30
minutes or until fish flakes with fork. Sprinkle with ¼ cup parsley and additional paprika.

6 servings.

The Sporty Panfish

For the cook...

Various sunfish, rock bass and crappie all fit into a skillet—even when they've reached their adult length, hence the name "panfish". They're caught more frequently than any other type of fish, offering fine sport as well as a good time in the kitchen and a great taste experience on the table. Sautéing is a natural way of preparing these fish. They are delicious cooked in a little butter, seasoned olive oil or peanut oil. Other techniques to try are pan frying, deep frying, grilling, baking or broiling. These little fish are generally scaled; their skin cooks up crisp and is pleasurable to the taste.

For the angler...

Because panfish are generally easier to find and more abundant than other fish, they offer a good opportunity to try new angling techniques. As Mr. Meinerding's story reveals, creativity is as essential to fishing as the bait.

For us all...

Creative thinking inspires experimentation. Experiments bring discoveries. And discoveries bring good fortune.

One evening when I was a kid, my buddy and I decided to fish at the end of a long dock. We fired the lantern up and hung it out over the end of the dock. Then we baited our hooks with nightcrawlers, and there we sat, two poles a piece, watching our lines and waiting for the channel catfish to bite.

The minute I changed rigs and tried a bobber it was gone. To my surprise it was a nice crappie. I put him in the bucket and tossed my line back in. Bam! Another crappie! By this time, my friend was rigging one of his poles with a bobber. By morning we had our limit of beautiful crappies.

That night took place almost 20 years ago.

Since then I have figured it out. The light drew the bugs. The bugs dropping in the water drew the minnows. The minnows drew the crappies. And the waves bouncing our baits up and down drew the bites. I still use that trick with a light, but I've learned that a jig-and-minnow makes a better bait.

Herb Meinerding, Jr.
Winchester, IN

*Roast sweet potatoes over the campfire or in your oven
on a crisp fall night, then, in the morning, make pancakes
with the roasted sweet potatoes. Stack them high with thyme-seasoned sunfish.*

Sweet Potato Cakes Stacked with Panfish

SWEET POTATO CAKES

3 to 4 roasted sweet potatoes
1 tablespoon pure maple syrup
1 teaspoon finely grated fresh ginger root
½ teaspoon salt
¼ teaspoon pepper
2 tablespoons butter

CRAPPIE

4 crappie (about 8-10 ounces each), cleaned
⅓ cup flour
2 teaspoons chopped fresh thyme leaves
¼ teaspoon salt
¼ teaspoon pepper
2 tablespoons butter

Prepare grill or wood fire: heat until coals are ash white or a wood fire has burned down to coals.

Prepare the sweet potato cakes: combine all potato cake ingredients except butter. Form into 8 cakes. Melt 1 tablespoon butter in large skillet; place 4 cakes in pan. Cook cakes over medium-hot coals for 3 to 4 minutes on each side. Repeat with remaining cakes. Keep warm.

Make the fish: clean, wash and pat fish dry. Combine all crappie ingredients except butter. Roll fish in flour mixture; tap off excess flour. Place 2 crappie in large skillet. Fry fish in 1 tablespoon butter over medium-hot coals, about 4 minutes on each side. Fry until fish is firm to the touch and golden brown. Repeat with remaining fish.

To dine, place fish between 2 cakes and serve with syrup.

4 servings.

Coat panfish in a chili powder and cornmeal crust, then cook in a skillet
with poblano chile peppers and sunny-side-up eggs.
This can be an anglers breakfast or supper during the spring season opener.

Sunnies-Side-Up with Eggs

SUNFISH
4 sunfish (about 8-10 ounces each), cleaned
¼ cup flour
¼ cup stone ground cornmeal
2 teaspoons chili powder
½ teaspoon cumin powder
½ teaspoon salt
¼ teaspoon coarse ground pepper
2 tablespoons chile infused oil
2 poblano chile peppers, seeded, cut into ½-inch pieces

EGGS
4 fresh eggs
¼ teaspoon chili powder
¼ teaspoon salt
¼ teaspoon coarse ground pepper

Prepare grill or wood fire: heat until coals are ash white or a wood fire has
burned down to coals.

Prepare the fish: clean, wash and pat fish dry. Combine all sunfish ingredients
except chile peppers. Roll fish in cornmeal mixture; tap off excess cornmeal.
Place 2 sunfish in large skillet. Fry fish and half of peppers in 1 tablespoon oil
over medium-hot coals, about 4 minutes on each side. Fry until fish is firm to
the touch and golden brown. Repeat with remaining fish. Keep warm.

Make the eggs: in same skillet, prepare sunny-side up eggs seasoned with chili
powder, salt and pepper. Scrambled, poached or over-easy eggs can also be
prepared.

To dine, present fish and eggs on individual plates; sprinkle with chiles and
coarse ground pepper.

4 servings.

Brown the panfish while eggs cook with spinach and pieces
of sun-dried tomatoes. Serve on sourdough toast. Make sun-dried tomatoes
at the campsite or in your backyard, simply baking them in the summer sun.

Sun-Dried Tomatoes
with Spinach and Panfish

BLUEGILL

4 bluegill (about 8-10 ounces
each), cleaned

⅓ cup flour

¼ cup finely grated
Parmesan cheese

½ teaspoon coarse
ground pepper

¼ teaspoon coarse salt

2 tablespoons olive oil

SCRAMBLED EGGS

8 eggs, slightly beaten

¼ teaspoon coarse ground pepper

2 teaspoons olive oil

2 cups fresh spinach leaves, torn

¼ cup coarsely chopped
sun-dried tomatoes

½ cup crumbled feta cheese

Prepare grill or wood fire: heat until coals are ash white or a wood fire has
burned down to coals.

Prepare the fish: clean, wash and pat fish dry. Combine all bluegill ingredients
except olive oil. Roll fish in flour mixture; tap off excess flour. Place 2 bluegills
in large skillet. Fry fish in 1 tablespoon oil over medium-hot coals, about 4 minutes on each side. Fry until fish is firm to the touch and golden brown. Repeat
with remaining fish. Keep warm.

Make the eggs: beat eggs with ¼ teaspoon pepper in medium bowl. Heat olive
oil in skillet; pour in eggs. Cook eggs over medium-hot coals, turning occasionally, until eggs are set and scrambled. Add spinach, tomatoes and feta cheese.
Continue to cook until spinach is wilted.

To dine, place fish on top of each serving of scrambled eggs.

4 servings.

Eggs, onions and curry are scrambled together while the fish pan-fries.
The curry spice warms a winter's morning.

Curried Eggs and Panfish

CRAPPIE

4 crappie (about 8-10 ounces each), cleaned
⅓ cup flour
1 tablespoon curry powder
1 teaspoon dried thyme leaves
½ teaspoon salt
½ teaspoon coarse ground pepper
2 tablespoons sesame oil

SCRAMBLED EGGS

1 tablespoon sesame oil
2 sweet onions, sliced
8 eggs, slightly beaten
1 teaspoon tumeric
½ teaspoon dried thyme leaves
¼ teaspoon salt
¼ teaspoon pepper

Prepare grill or wood fire: heat until coals are ash white or a wood fire has burned down to coals.

Prepare the fish: clean, wash and pat fish dry. Combine all crappie ingredients except oil. Roll fish in flour mixture; tap off excess flour. Place 2 crappie in large skillet. Fry fish in 1 tablespoon oil over medium-hot coals, about 4 minutes on each side. Fry until fish is firm to the touch and golden brown. Repeat with remaining fish. Keep warm.

Make the eggs: heat oil in skillet; add onions. Cook onions over medium-hot coals, stirring occasionally, for 6 to 8 minutes or until onions are tender. Stir in eggs and seasonings. Cook eggs, turning occasionally, until eggs are set and scrambled.

To dine, place fish on top of each serving of scrambled eggs.

4 servings.

Cook lentils with bacon, tomatoes and onion. Pan-roast the panfish with
some of the bacon fat and serve with the lentils.

Panfish with Lentils and Bacon

4 strips bacon, cut crosswise into ½-inch pieces
1 medium onion, thinly sliced
2 carrots, sliced
1 stalk celery, sliced
2 cloves garlic, coarsely chopped
1 ¼ cup lentils
14 ½-ounce can chicken broth
1 cup canned crushed tomatoes in thick puree
1 teaspoon dried thyme leaves
½ teaspoon salt
½ teaspoon coarse ground pepper
2 bay leaves
1 tablespoon vegetable oil
4 crappie (about 8 ounces each)

Place the bacon in a medium saucepan. Cook over medium-high heat, stirring
occasionally, about 4 minutes or until browned. Pour off and reserve all but 2
tablespoons fat from the pan. Add onion, carrots, celery and garlic to bacon
drippings. Cook, stirring frequently, about 5 minutes or until vegetables are
browned. Add remaining ingredients except vegetable oil and fish. Bring to a
boil; reduce heat to low. Simmer, covered, about 30 minutes or until lentils are
tender. Measure reserved bacon drippings in skillet; add enough vegetable oil to
measure 2 tablespoons. Sauté fish in hot oil over high heat about 2 to 3 minutes
on each side or just until browned. Serve fish on lentils.

To drink, try a bottle of Pinot Noir.

4 servings.

Brush basil pesto on dressed crappie while grilling.
Serve the pesto crappie on a bed of tomato slices.

Pesto Crappie
with Tomato Slices

1/4 cup prepared basil pesto
8 (about 4-5 ounces each) crappie fillets
4 ripe tomatoes, sliced
2 tablespoons grated fresh Parmesan cheese
1/2 teaspoon coarse ground pepper

Prepare grill or wood fire: heat until coals are ash white or a wood fire has burned down to coals.

Place 4 fillets in large skillet; brush with 2 tablespoons pesto. Fry fish over medium-hot coals, about 2 minutes on each side. Fry until fish flakes with a fork. Repeat with remaining fish.

To dine, slice tomatoes on individual plates; place 2 fillets on bed of tomatoes. Sprinkle with Parmesan cheese and pepper.

4 servings.

Panfish seasoned with olive oil, sage and rosemary is sprinkled
with vinegar, coarse salt and pepper.

Tuscan Grilled Panfish

¼ cup olive oil
2 cloves garlic, thinly sliced
1 teaspoon finely chopped fresh sage leaves
1 teaspoon finely chopped fresh rosemary leaves
2 tablespoons red wine vinegar
½ teaspoon coarse salt
½ teaspoon coarse ground pepper
4 panfish (about 2 pounds), cleaned, scaled

Prepare grill or wood fire: heat until coals are ash white or a wood fire has
burned down to coals.

Place oil, garlic, sage and rosemary in small saucepan. Cook over medium-low
heat about 2 minutes or just until garlic begins to brown. Remove from heat,
immediately stir in vinegar and ¼ teaspoon each of salt and pepper. Place panfish in glass pan; pour half of the vinegar mixture over fish. Turn fish to coat.
Sprinkle with remaining salt and pepper. Place fish on oiled grate of grill. Grill
over medium-hot coals about 4 minutes on each side or until fish flakes with
fork. Whisk remaining vinegar mixture; serve over grilled fish.

To drink, Try a Pinot Grigio or Soave.

4 servings.

Grapefruit and lime juice
serve as both marinade and dressing for broiled fish.

Sunfish with Red Onion and Citrus

¼ cup olive oil
2 tablespoons fresh grapefruit juice
2 tablespoons fresh lime juice
2 tablespoons snipped fresh chives
4 panfish (about 2 pounds), cleaned, scaled
1 medium red onion, thinly sliced
½ teaspoon coarse salt
½ teaspoon coarse ground pepper

Combine olive oil, grapefruit juice, lime juice and 1 tablespoon chives in small bowl. Place panfish in glass pan; pour half of the dressing over fish; place onion over the top.

Let stand for 10 minutes. Heat broiler; place fish on greased broiler pan. Broil fish about 6 to 8 inches from heat, turning after 4 minutes. Brush with marinade from pan.

Sprinkle with salt and pepper. Broil about 3 minutes or until fish flakes with fork. Serve fish with remaining dressing (which you should bring to boil before serving); sprinkle with remaining chives.

To dine, place grapefruit wedges and avocado around fish.

4 servings.

Dried cherries, currants and apricots
season couscous that are cooked
in the pan drippings of herb-coated fish.

Panfish with Fruited Couscous

2 tablespoons olive oil
4 bluegill (about 6 ounces each), cleaned, scaled
2 cloves garlic, coarsely chopped
2 teaspoons chopped fresh rosemary leaves
½ teaspoon salt
¼ teaspoon pepper
8 ounce package (about 1 cup) couscous
1 cup mixture of currants, dried cherries and chopped dried apricots

Heat oil over medium-high heat in a large skillet; place bluegill in skillet. Season with garlic, rosemary, salt and pepper. Sauté for 3 minutes on each side, or until fish flakes with fork. Remove from pan; keep warm. In same skillet with pan drippings, prepare couscous according to package directions. Stir in dried fruit.

To dine, serve fish on bed of couscous.

4 servings.

*Pan-fry cloves of garlic with crappie. Toast crusty
bread in the pan, then stack the crappie on this
bread with tomatoes, basil leaves and the garlic chips.*

Garlic Chip Crappie Sandwiches

¼ cup olive oil
12 cloves garlic, cut into thin slices
½ cup torn basil leaves
8 (about 4-5 ounces each) crappie fillets
½ teaspoon coarse salt
½ teaspoon coarse ground pepper
8 slices crusty sourdough bread
2 ripe tomatoes, sliced
Basil leaves

Combine olive oil and garlic in small saucepan. Cook over low heat, stirring occasionally, about 8 to 10 minutes or until garlic just starts to brown. Strain the oil; reserve garlic chips. Stir torn basil leaves into oil. Pour 1 tablespoons basil oil into large skillet. Place 4 crappie fillets in pan; season with ¼ teaspoon each salt and pepper. Sauté over medium-high heat, about 3 minutes on each side or until fish flakes with fork. Remove from pan; keep warm. Repeat with remaining fillets.

Meanwhile, brush bread with basil oil. Toast in oven or broiler. Stack each slice of toast with 2 tomato slices, 2 basil leaves and 1 crappie fillet. Top with garlic chips.

To dine, serve sandwiches with salad greens and goat cheese.

4 servings.

Salsa verde is an Italian sauce
made with capers, parsley and anchovies.
Rub this sauce on panfish before pan grilling.
Drizzle the remaining sauce over the panfish
and serve with avocado.

Grilled Panfish with Salsa Verde

12 medium tomatillos, removed from skin
1 ripe tomato
¼ cup chopped fresh cilantro
Juice of 2 limes
1 tablespoon olive oil
¼ cup sliced green onions
¼ teaspoon salt
4 sunfish (about 8-10 ounces each), cleaned, scaled

Prepare grill or wood fire: heat until coals are ash white or a wood fire has burned down to coals. Place tomatillos and tomato on oiled grate of grill. Grill over medium-hot coals about 5 minutes or until tomatillos begin to char. Chop grilled tomatillos and tomato; in medium bowl add cilantro, lime juice and olive oil to chopped tomatoes. Stir in green onions and salt. Place sunfish on grill. Grill over medium coals about 4 minutes. Turn fish; spoon 2 tablespoons tomato mixture on each fish. Continue to grill about 4 minutes or until fish flakes with fork. Serve salsa verde with fish.

4 servings.

Bake the fish with tomatoes, corn and celery.
The spice is hot pepper sauce, dry mustard and thyme.

Panfish Creole

2 tablespoons butter
2 onions, coarsely chopped
2 green peppers, coarsely chopped
2 stalks celery, sliced
4 cloves garlic, coarsely chopped
6 ripe tomatoes, chopped
1 bay leaf
2 teaspoons dried thyme leaves
2 teaspoons dried basil leaves
1 teaspoon cayenne pepper
14 ½-ounce can chicken broth
10-ounce package frozen corn
8 (about 4-5 ounces each) panfish fillets
½ teaspoon salt
½ teaspoon coarse ground pepper
1 teaspoon hot pepper sauce

Heat butter in large skillet until sizzling. Add onions, green peppers, celery and garlic. Sauté over medium-high heat, stirring occasionally, about 5 minutes or until vegetables begin to brown. Add tomatoes, bay leaf, thyme, basil and pepper. Reduce heat to medium, cook for 10 minutes to blend flavors. Stir in chicken broth and corn. Pour into 13 x 9-inch baking dish; top with panfish fillets. Season with salt, pepper and hot pepper sauce. Bake at 375°F for 12 to 15 minutes or until fish flakes with fork. Sprinkle with additional dried basil leaves.

6 servings.

Brush this New Orleans barbecue sauce
(that is spiced and not sweet) on broiled crappie.

Barbecued Crappie

1 teaspoon cayenne pepper
1 teaspoon coarse ground pepper
½ teaspoon salt
½ teaspoon crushed red pepper
½ teaspoon dried thyme leaves
½ teaspoon dried rosemary leaves, crushed
¼ teaspoon dried oregano leaves
8 (about 4-5 ounces each) crappie fillets
¼ cup unsalted butter
3 cloves garlic, coarsely chopped
1 teaspoon Worcestershire sauce
½ cup beer at room temperature

Combine cayenne pepper, pepper, salt, red pepper, thyme, rosemary and oregano in small pan. Coat both sides of crappie fillets with seasoning. Melt butter in large skillet until sizzling; stir in remaining seasoning mixture, garlic and Worcestershire sauce. Place crappie fillets in skillet. Cook over medium heat, about 3 minutes on each side or until fish flakes with fork. Stir in beer. Continue cooking, about 2 minutes or until beer is simmering.

6 servings.

The Perfect Perch

For the cook...

Perch love a variety of waters, and are native to large and clear northern lakes with clean, sandy bottoms. But stocking has carried them near and far, and no matter where you find them, weedbeds and their edges are perch magnets. Why? Because that's where perch food—minnows and crustaceans—congregate. Perch are schooling fish, and where you catch one you should be able to get enough in your basket for a campground fish fry. Yellow Perch are "perfect" because they're willing biters *and* because their mild flavor—equal to walleye in every respect—is perfect on the table.

For the angler...

Perch are not necessarily thought of as the most glamorous sporting fish in fresh water, but they certainly are fun to catch. Isn't that part of what fishing is all about anyway? And the action can be fast and furious, as attested to in Mr. Carpenter's story.

For us all...

In fishing, as in life, it's okay to occasionally just go somewhere and have good, plain, old-fashioned fun without any "agendas" guiding our actions. Plus, given fishing's modern catch-and-release ethic, it's fun to be able to walk off a lake with a bucket of perch to enjoy on the dinner table. Fishing like that is harder and harder to find these days, as are simple times that are just plain relaxing ...

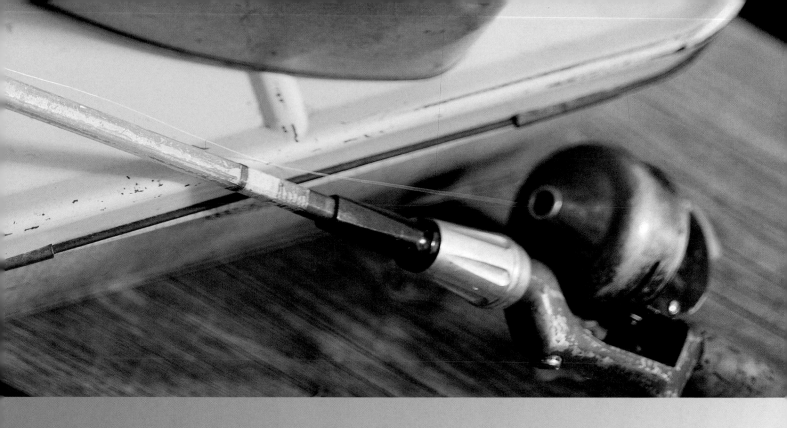

By mid-March, the ice was getting honeycombed on our central Minnesota lakes, but in the far northwoods, several feet of thick, safe ice still locked in the lakes. So we headed to Winnibigoshish, a huge Mississippi River reservoir. Despite the ice, the perch knew Spring was coming, and we sat out there in sweatshirts in the warm sun, pulling in perch after perch: some fairly good-sized, all fillet-able. Usually, you would have two fish on at once, if you could even get a second rod, baited with minnow, in the water. Where were they? Staging for spawning, just out from the bulrush flats, in only 5 or 6 feet of water. The bobber would just keep going down as soon as it hit the water! Our group caught hundreds of handsome, yellow-green-orange perch in the two days we were there, getting our faces sunburned from the sunlight reflecting up off the ice, but we were too busy having fun to notice. Perch saved the day, bringing us out of our winter doldrums.

Tom Carpenter
Plymouth, MN

Grill sourdough bread with olive oil. Brush fish
with summer's best pesto, tomatoes and basil
leaves. Stack it all on the grilled bread.

Pesto and Tomato Fish Bruschetta

8 (about 4 ounces each) perch fillets
2 tablespoons prepared pesto
4 slices sourdough bread, cut ½-inch thick
2 tablespoons olive oil
¼ teaspoon coarse salt
¼ teaspoon coarse ground pepper
2 ripe tomatoes, sliced
8 basil leaves

Prepare grill or wood fire: heat until coals are ash white or a wood fire has burned down to coals. Place fillets on oiled grill rack; brush with pesto. Grill over medium-hot coals, about 2 minutes. Turn fillets; brush with additional pesto. Place bread around the fillets; brush with olive oil. Grill fillets and bread about 2 minutes or until fish flakes with a fork and bread is toasted. Sprinkle bread with salt and pepper.

To dine, stack bruschetta with tomato slices, fish fillets and 2 basil leaves.

4 servings.

Make springtime cucumbers and red onions into a slaw,
and use it to top a broiled fish fillet on rye bread.

Open-Faced Fish Sandwich with Cucumber Slaw

CUCUMBER SLAW

2 medium cucumbers, coarsely chopped
1 medium red onion, coarsely chopped
2 tablespoons sour cream
1 tablespoon prepared horseradish
1/4 teaspoon salt
1/4 teaspoon pepper

PERCH

8 (about 4 ounces each) perch fillets
1/4 teaspoon salt
1/4 teaspoon pepper
2 tablespoons orange juice
4 slices rye bread

Make the slaw: combine all slaw ingredients in medium bowl. Let stand 30 minutes or cover and refrigerate.

Prepare the fish: heat broiler; place fish on greased broiler pan. Season with salt and pepper; brush with 1 tablespoon orange juice. Broil fish 6 to 8 inches from heat, turning after 3 minutes. Brush with remaining orange juice; broil about 3 minutes or until fish flakes with fork. Toast bread under the broiler.

To dine, place fish fillets on toasted rye. Spoon slaw over the sandwich.

4 servings.

The best peaches are usually picked in the fall.
Season peaches with lime and sweet onion.
Grill the fish with the peaches, serve the fish and the peaches
in sliced French or sourdough rolls with tartar sauce.

Peach Fisherman's Sandwich

1 tablespoon butter
8 (about 4 ounces each) perch fillets
1 sweet onion, sliced
½ teaspoon salt
½ teaspoon coarse ground pepper
2 ripe peaches, pitted, sliced
2 tablespoons fresh lime juice
4 French or sourdough rolls, split
Horseradish mayonnaise

Prepare grill or wood fire: heat until coals are ash white or a wood fire has burned down to coals. Heat butter in large skillet over medium-hot coals until sizzling. Add fish fillets and onion. Sprinkle with salt and pepper. Fry fish, about 2 minutes on each side. Fry until fish flakes with fork. Remove fish from pan. Add peaches and lime juice to same pan. Grill, stirring occasionally, for 5 to 7 minutes or until peaches begin to caramelize.

To dine, spread French rolls with horseradish mayonnaise; fill with fish fillets and peaches.

4 servings.

Layer grilled fish, peppers and salami between slices of crusty herb bread.
Olives, capers and marinated artichokes are the condiments for this sandwich
that is welcome during the winter months.

Antipasto Sandwich

8 (about 4 ounces each) perch fillets
2 red peppers, cut into wedges
1 sweet onion, thinly sliced
2 tablespoons caper Italian dressing
8 slices crusty herb bread
8 thin slices hard salami

Prepare grill or wood fire: heat until coals are ash white or a wood fire has
burned down to coals. Place fillets on greased grate of grill. Place peppers and
onion around fillets; brush with dressing. Grill over medium-hot coals, about 3
minutes on each side or until fish flakes with fork. Place bread on grill; grill for
2 to 3 minutes or until toasted.

Stack sandwiches with 1 slice toasted bread, roasted pepper, onion and 2 slices
salami. Top with remaining toasted bread.

To dine, serve sandwiches with marinated artichokes, olives and capers.

4 servings.

Onion, garlic, cayenne pepper and other spices are the jerk seasonings for broiled fish.

Jerk Seasoned Perch

½ cup chopped onion
2 cloves garlic, coarsely chopped
2 teaspoons brown sugar
2 teaspoons ground allspice
2 teaspoons dried thyme leaves
1 teaspoon salt
½ teaspoon coarse ground pepper
½ teaspoon nutmeg
¼ teaspoon cayenne pepper
8 (about 4 ounces each) perch fillets
1 teaspoon vinegar

Purée all ingredients except perch fillets and vinegar in food processor or blender container. Coat both sides of perch fillets with jerk mixture. Heat broiler; place fish skin side down on greased broiler pan. Sprinkle remaining seasoning over fish. Broil fish 6 to 8 inches from heat, about 5 minutes or until golden brown. Drizzle with vinegar.

4 servings.

The Noble Salmon

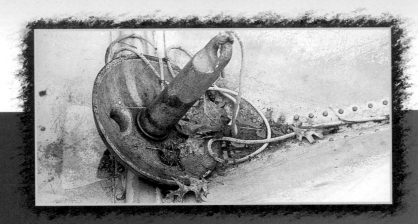

For the cook...

Salmon are symbols of the wild—they are roamers that bring their distinctive flavor to the table. Salmon tastes as wild and wonderful as the places you catch them. This noble fish—perfect in form, splendid in texture and succulent in taste—is delicious off the grill, or chilled and served with the freshest of garden vegetables. Salmon is easy to prepare whole, filleted or as steaks. Salmon's firm, distinct flavor is delicious poached, grilled, broiled, baked or sautéed.

For the angler...

Fishermen travel throughout the continent in pursuit of the adventure provided by Atlantic, chinook (king), coho, red and other members of the salmon family. Mr. Schoenlein's account of salmon fishing in Alaska reminds us how sensational an experience fishing can be.

For us all...

In the salmon expedition, determination binds the angler to his catch with a single-minded focus worthy of all great warriors. A fixed movement toward the object of prey closes the gap between the hunter and the hunted. Locked in battle, lost in the moment, the determined fisherman allows no distractions. Only victory or defeat breaks the spell.

Being confined to a wheelchair it is hard to get out in the rugged Alaska country. I was lucky in that my nephew Nick, a resident of the area, knew the good spots.

The river was full of Alaskan kings. My fishing companions and I were fishing with spinning gear, drifting streamers. I had hand-tied the streamers, and did they work! On my first hit a king tested my drag. It had to weigh about 70 pounds. It took off downriver, jumping like a bucking horse. I felt three hard tugs and the line snapped. I loosened my drag and tied on another streamer. In front of me, I could see nothing but a large red reflection in the water. While reeling in my streamer, that red reflection took off after my bait. Was that a big fish! It had to be close to 100 pounds. It took off down the river like the last one and with the same result.

The next day I came back with determination. I had 12 lb. test on my spinning reel and a medium-sized rod. Once again the river was full of kings. I cast my line up stream, watching the line drift with the current. Once it stopped I set the hook. And the fight was on. It took a full 30 minutes to bring it in. The king was about 3 feet long and weighed around 40 pounds. That was my first Alaskan king.

Kenneth Schoenlein
Willow, AK

*Savory herbs and wonderful salmon come together
in a summer delight.*

Herbed Tomato Vinaigrette Salmon

2 ripe tomatoes, chopped
1 red onion, chopped
2 tablespoons red wine vinegar
2 tablespoons olive oil
1 tablespoon Dijon-style mustard
1 tablespoon capers, slightly crushed
½ teaspoon coarse ground pepper
3-4 pound salmon fillet
½ cup mixture of chopped basil leaves
¼ teaspoon coarse salt

Prepare grill or wood fire: heat until coals are ash white or a wood fire has burned down to coals.

Meanwhile, combine tomatoes, onion, vinegar, oil, mustard, capers and pepper. Place salmon, skin-side down, on oiled grill rack over medium-hot coals. Spoon tomato mixture on salmon, (reserve remaining tomatoes). Grill for about 20 minutes or until fish flakes with fork. Sprinkle with basil and salt.

To dine, present salmon on bed of tomato slices with a splash of vinegar. Garnish with basil leaves.

8 to 10 servings.

In the autumn, when peppers are at their bounty,
prepare salmon with a kalamata olive spread.
Roast peppers around the salmon on the grill.

Roasted Peppers with Salmon

1 tablespoon olive oil
1 tablespoon balsamic vinegar
¼ cup kalamata olive spread
1 teaspoon chopped fresh rosemary leaves
3-4 pound salmon fillet
3 sweet and hot peppers, red, poblano,
or Hungarian, seeded and cut into wedges
Fresh ground pepper

Prepare grill or wood fire: heat until coals are ash white or a wood fire has burned down to coals.

Meanwhile, combine oil, vinegar, olive spread and rosemary. Place salmon, skin-side down, on oiled grill rack over medium-hot coals. Brush olive mixture on salmon. Place peppers around salmon. Grill for about 10 minutes or until peppers are blackened. Turn peppers, grill about 10 minutes or until fish flakes with fork. Sprinkle with fresh ground pepper.

To dine, present salmon with roasted peppers and kalamata olives.

8 to 10 servings.

*Sauté grated fresh ginger root, lemon, watercress and sweet onions
together, and place on a three- to four-pound salmon fillet.
Grill this salmon and serve chilled for spring gatherings.
The salmon also travels well to the lake for fishing outings and other adventures.*

Grilled Salmon with Spring Herbs

1 tablespoon olive oil
1 sweet onion, chopped
1 bulb fennel, chopped
½ cup fennel weed
1 tablespoon finely grated ginger root
3 garlic cloves, finely chopped
2 teaspoons grated lemon peel
2 tablespoons lemon juice
½ cup chopped watercress
3-4 pounds salmon fillet
½ teaspoon coarse salt
½ teaspoon coarse ground pepper

Prepare grill or wood fire: heat until coals are ash white or a wood fire has burned down to coals.

Meanwhile, heat oil over medium heat. Add onion, fennel, fennel weed, ginger root and garlic. Sauté, stirring occasionally, for 4 to 5 minutes or until vegetables are tender. Sprinkle salmon with lemon peel and lemon juice; let stand for 10 minutes. Mix watercress with onion mixture. Place salmon, skin side down, on oiled grill rack over medium-hot coals. Spoon onion mixture on salmon (reserve remaining herbs).

Grill for about 20 minutes or until fish flakes with fork. Sprinkle with any remaining herbs, salt and pepper.

To dine, present salmon on bed of field greens, watercress and arugula. Garnish with spring radishes and onions.

8 to 10 servings.

Blood orange and zest of lemon are the 10-minute marinade for salmon.
Serve this grilled salmon with winter citrus wedges of blood orange, grapefruit and orange.
A salad of field greens and gorgonzola cheese completes this wintry meal.

Citrus Marinated Salmon

Juice of 2 blood oranges
Zest of 1 lemon
1 tablespoon olive oil
1 teaspoon chopped fresh sage leaves
3-4 pound salmon fillet
½ teaspoon coarse salt
½ teaspoon coarse ground pepper

Prepare grill or wood fire: heat until coals are ash white or a wood fire has burned down to coals.

Meanwhile, combine juice, lemon zest, oil and sage leaves in small bowl. Place salmon in large glass pan; pour over marinade. Let stand 10 minutes. Place salmon, skin-side down, on oiled grill rack over medium-hot coals. Grill for about 20 minutes or until fish flakes with fork. Sprinkle with salt and pepper.

To dine, present salmon with grilled citrus wedges. Sprinkle with crumbled gorgonzola or bleu cheese.

8 to 10 servings.

Poach salmon in an herb broth.
Serve chilled salmon on a bed of yellow tomatoes
with a dressing made from tomatoes, shallots and mint.

Poached Salmon with Cucumber Sauce.

SALMON

1 ½ quarts water

1 ½ cups dry white wine

3 tablespoons white wine vinegar

1 onion, sliced

1 carrot, sliced

6 sprigs fresh parsley

2 sprigs fresh thyme

5 peppercorns

3 bay leaves

2 pounds center-cut salmon fillet,
cut into 4 pieces

1 teaspoon coarse salt

CUCUMBER SAUCE

2 cucumbers, peeled,
seeded and grated

½ teaspoon coarse salt

2 cups plain yogurt

¼ cup chopped
fresh mint leaves

1 clove garlic, finely chopped

½ teaspoon coarse
ground pepper

Prepare the fish: combine all salmon ingredients except salmon and salt in large, deep skillet. Cover; bring to a boil over high heat. Reduce heat and simmer, partially covered for about 10 minutes. Sprinkle salmon with salt; add fillets to liquid in pan. Bring back to a simmer. Simmer, partially covered, about 4 minutes or until the fish is just barely done. Remove the pan from the heat; let fillets stand in liquid for about 2 minutes or until fish flakes with fork. Serve the salmon at room temperature with cucumber sauce.

Make the cucumber sauce: combine the cucumbers with the salt. Let stand for 10 minutes. With your hands, squeeze the cucumbers and discard the liquid. Stir together drained cucumbers and remaining cucumber sauce ingredients. Refrigerate until ready to serve.

To dine, place salmon on individual serving plates and spoon sauce over salmon. Garnish with cucumber slices and mint.

4 servings.

Sauté salmon steaks with baby spinach leaves, tomatoes and feta cheese.

Spinach and Feta
Sautéed with Salmon Steaks

1 tablespoon olive oil
4 salmon steaks, (about 1-inch thick)
2 tablespoons capers, slightly crushed
3 cups baby spinach leaves
1 medium tomato, coarsely chopped
½ teaspoon coarse salt
½ teaspoon coarse ground pepper
⅓ cup crumbled feta cheese

Heat oil in large skillet over medium-high heat. Place steaks in skillet; sprinkle with capers. Sauté, about 3 minutes on each side, or until browned. Gradually add spinach leaves, allowing them to wilt down. Add tomato, salt and pepper. Cook for about 2 minutes or until spinach is completely wilted. Sprinkle with feta cheese.

4 servings.

Sauté salmon steaks with lemons, garlic and butter
until the lemons and butter caramelize. Cooking the lemons slowly
brings out the natural sugar content,
creating a golden, caramel color and sweet flavor.

Caramelized Lemons and Caper Salmon Steaks

1 tablespoon butter
2 lemons, sliced
2 tablespoons capers
2 cloves garlic, coarsely chopped
4 salmon steaks, (about 1-inch thick)
¼ teaspoon coarse salt
¼ teaspoon coarse ground pepper

Heat butter over medium heat until sizzling; add lemon slices, capers and garlic.

Cook lemons, turning occasionally, for about 5 to 7 minutes or until caramelized.

Remove from pan; set aside. In same skillet, place salmon steaks; season with salt and pepper. Sauté over medium-high heat, about 4 minutes on each side, or until fish flakes with fork. Add caramelized lemon mixture.

4 servings.

Baste pan-seared salmon steaks with a rice wine vinegar and chile pepper sauce.
A minted date chutney complements the salmon. Simply serve with rice and crackers.

Seared Salmon Steaks
with Minted Chutney

MINTED CHUTNEY
4 cups packed mint leaves
2 jalapeños, seeds removed
¼ cup grated unsweetened coconut
8 pitted dates
½ cup fresh lime juice
½ cup fresh orange juice

SALMON
1 cup rice wine vinegar
3 tablespoons dry masala wine
1 tablespoon sugar
1 teaspoon coarse salt
1 teaspoon paprika
½ teaspoon chile flakes
4 salmon steaks, (about 1 ¼-inch thick)

Prepare grill or wood fire: heat until coals are ash white or a wood fire has burned down to coals.

Make the chutney: combine all ingredients in a food processor or blender. Process about 3 minutes or until smooth. Refrigerate until serving.

Prepare the fish: combine all ingredients except salmon in a small bowl. Place salmon steaks in plastic food bag. Pour in marinade; seal tightly. Place in 13 x 9-inch pan; let stand for 15 minutes. Place steaks on oiled grate of grill. Grill over medium-hot coals about 5 minutes on each side or until fish flakes with fork.

To dine, serve salmon steaks with chutney. Sprinkle with additional unsweetened coconut and a sprig of mint.

4 servings.

Bake salmon with cannellini beans, tomato wedges and basil.

Salmon with Cannellini Beans

3 cups cooked cannellini beans
1 medium red onion, sliced
1 tablespoon olive oil
1 tablespoon white wine vinegar
2 pounds center-cut salmon fillet, cut into 4 pieces
$\frac{1}{2}$ teaspoon coarse salt
$\frac{1}{2}$ teaspoon coarse ground pepper
2 ripe tomatoes, cut into wedges
$\frac{1}{2}$ cup chopped fresh basil leaves

Combine beans, onion, oil and vinegar; spoon into 9-inch casserole dish. Place salmon fillets on beans; season with salt and pepper. Bake at 375°F for 15 minutes; add tomato wedges. Bake for 5 minutes or until tomatoes are heated through. Stir in basil.

4 servings.

Season a whole salmon lightly with salt, ginger,
scallions and sesame oil. Then poach or steam the fish in lemon water.

Steamed Salmon
with Scallions and Ginger

5 pound whole salmon, cleaned, head removed

Sea salt

¼ cup grated fresh ginger root

¼ cup soy sauce

¼ cup dry sherry

2 teaspoons Asian sesame oil

2 lemons, thinly sliced

16 green onions, halved crosswise,
finely julienned and cut in 1-inch pieces

Clean, wash and pat dry fish. Make 6 parallel diagonal 2-inch-long slashes on each side of the fish, slicing through to the bone. Rub the fish with sea salt. In a mortar, pound the ginger to a paste with ¼ teaspoon salt. Stuff one-third of the ginger paste into each slash in fish. Mix the remaining two-thirds of the ginger paste with soy sauce, sherry and sesame oil. Spoon the sauce into the cavity and on the top of the fish. Tuck half of the onions into slashes. Let stand for 15 to 20 minutes. Fill large steam pan with about 1 gallon water. Cover; bring to a boil over high heat. Reduce heat and simmer, partially covered for about 10 minutes. Add lemon slices. Place salmon in water; bring back to simmer. Simmer, partially covered, about 30 to 40 minutes or until fish flakes with fork. Remove the pan from the heat; remove salmon.

Sprinkle with remaining onions and a little salt. Refrigerate until serving time.

To dine, present fish with salad greens, lemons and melon.

12 servings.

Skewer pieces of salmon with slices of fennel bulb
and wedges of orange. Then grill or broil.

Salmon Kabobs
with Fennel

2 fennel bulbs, each cut into 8 wedges, reserve fennel weed
2 pounds salmon, cut into 1 ½-inch pieces
2 oranges, each cut into 8 wedges
2 teaspoons grated orange peel
½ cup fresh orange juice
1 tablespoon vegetable oil
2 teaspoons fennel seeds
½ teaspoon coarse salt
½ teaspoon coarse ground pepper

Prepare grill or wood fire: heat until coals are ash white or a wood fire has
burned down to coals. Meanwhile, thread each of 8 metal skewers alternately
with fennel, salmon and oranges. Combine remaining ingredients and ¼ cup
chopped fennel weed in small bowl. Marinate kabobs in orange juice mixture
about 10 minutes. Place kabobs on oiled grate of grill. Grill over medium-hot
coals about 5 minutes. Brush with remaining marinade. Turn kabobs; continue
grilling about 5 minutes or until fish flakes with fork.

8 servings.

The Running Steelhead

For the cook...

Steelhead are indigenous to the Pacific Ocean and are seagoing river runners related to rainbow trout. Steelhead, really rainbow trout that grow up in the sea (or, as can also be the case now, a Great Lake), live to spawn more than once. Their flesh is as orange and oily as any salmon and can be prepared with any of the salmon recipes as well.

For the angler...

For the novice, catching steelhead can be tricky. But with the aid of an experienced mentor, as Mr. Diaz' story shows, anything is possible. His story reveals that bounty comes from the heart as well as the net—no matter what kind of fishing we pursue.

For us all...

Formed around a shared passion, bonded through shared experience, and strengthened through mutual gain, camaraderie between anglers remains the unspoken treasure of this sport. To be introduced to a comrade's favorite fishing hole is the ultimate honor borne of trust.

Having only been fishing for a short time, I was blessed by having two great mentors who taught me how to fish for steelhead and salmon on the Reach (Columbia River). My apprenticeship on the mighty Columbia River was an enjoyable learning experience! I learned to watch my rod tip for the right action, as a fish won't hit a plug dragging foreign matter. I was shown how to properly sharpen my hooks. My friends instructed me in navigating the river, and imparted their secrets as to where to find the fish. They mentored me in preparing the catch of the day, smoking techniques and so much more. I feel tremendous gratitude for the generosity and patience of the friends who went out of their way to instruct me in the details of my new found passion.

That October morning we launched at 6:30 a.m. I felt certain one of the three fishermen in my boat was going to catch something. Sure enough, with the wind ripping at 35 to 45 mph and my kicker motor grinding against the current and wind, I hooked a 28 lb. 12 oz. buck steelhead! My buddies and I netted the buck into the boat only after great fight. It turns out I had caught the heaviest fish of the day! The thrill of catching this fish will stay with me a long time.

Mario F. Diaz, Sr.
Richland, WA

Use a mixture of yogurt, cumin, tumeric, paprika
and cayenne as a marinade and basting sauce for summery steelhead.

Tandoori Fish Cakes

2 pounds steelhead fillets
1 egg, slightly beaten
2/3 cup coarse dry bread crumbs
1/4 cup sliced green onion
2 tablespoons plain yogurt
1 teaspoon cumin
1 teaspoon tumeric
1 teaspoon paprika
1/4 teaspoon cayenne pepper
1/4 teaspoon salt
2 tablespoons olive oil

Prepare grill or wood fire: heat until coals are ash white or a wood fire has
burned down to coals. Place fillets on oiled grill rack, grill over medium-hot
coals, about 4 minutes on each side or until fish flakes with fork. Combine fish
with remaining ingredients. Shape the fish mixture into 7 or 8 patties; place on
grill. Grill about 4 minutes on each side or until patties are firm to the touch
and golden brown.

To dine, place fish cakes on mint leaves and garnish with lemon wedges.

4 servings.

Welcome springtime with steelhead served with a sauce made with mayonnaise,
mustard, capers and cornichons.

Mustard Spiced Fish Cakes

2 pounds steelhead fillets
1 egg, slightly beaten
2/3 cup coarse dry bread crumbs
1/2 cup chopped cornichons or pickles
2 tablespoons mayonnaise
1 tablespoon capers, chopped
1 tablespoon Dijon-style mustard
2 teaspoons grated lemon peel
1/4 teaspoon salt
1/4 teaspoon pepper
1/4 cup butter

Steam the steelhead over moderate steam for 7 minutes. Drain off any excess liquid and combine the fish with the remaining ingredients. Shape the fish mixture into 7 or 8 patties. Melt 2 tablespoons butter in large skillet over medium heat until sizzling. Place 4 patties in skillet. Sauté, about 3 minutes on each side or until patties are firm to the touch and golden brown. Sauté remaining patties in remaining 2 tablespoon butter.

To dine, present fish cakes on individual plates with a mixture of mustard greens, watercress and arugula.

4 servings.

Form fish, onions, peppers and lemon into cakes.
Pan-sear and serve with a roasted autumn squash puree.

Fish Cakes with Roasted Squash Purée

SQUASH PUREE
2 cups roasted butternut, sweet dumpling or acorn squash
1 tablespoon grated fresh ginger root
1 tablespoon Dijon-style mustard
2 tablespoons chopped fresh cilantro
½ teaspoon salt
½ teaspoon pepper

STEELHEAD
2 pounds steelhead fillets
1 egg, slightly beaten
2 jalapeño chile peppers, seeded, finely chopped
⅔ cup coarse dry bread crumbs
½ cup finely chopped red onion
1 tablespoon grated fresh ginger root
2 teaspoon grated lemon peel
2 tablespoons mayonnaise
¼ cup butter

Make the squash purée: combine roasted squash and remaining purée ingredients in medium bowl. Cover and refrigerate. Squash can be made ahead and refrigerated for up to 3 days.

Prepare the fish: steam the steelhead over moderate steam for 7 minutes. Drain off any excess liquid and combine the fish with the remaining steelhead ingredients. Shape the fish mixture into 7 or 8 patties. Melt 2 tablespoons butter in large skillet over medium heat until sizzling. Place 4 patties in skillet. Sauté, about 3 minutes on each side or until patties are firm to the touch and golden brown. Repeat with remaining patties in remaining 2 tablespoons butter.

To dine, present fish cakes on individual plates with salad greens and 1 table-spoon squash purée.

4 servings.

Homemade mashed potatoes and sautéed salmon
make a welcome meal for the winter holidays.

Pan-Seared Fish Cakes
with Garlic Mashed Potatoes

GARLIC MASHED POTATOES

2 pounds medium red potatoes,
unpeeled, cut into large pieces

1 tablespoon butter

5 cloves garlic,
coarsely chopped

1 pint heavy cream

1 teaspoon coarse salt

1/2 teaspoon coarse
ground pepper

STEELHEAD

2 pounds steelhead fillets

1 egg, slightly beaten

2/3 cup coarse dry bread crumbs

1/2 cup finely chopped leeks

1/2 cup chopped fresh parsley

1/2 teaspoon coarse ground pepper

2 tablespoons mayonnaise

1 tablespoon Dijon-style mustard

2 teaspoons grated lemon peel

Make the mashed potatoes: place potatoes in a large saucepan, cover with cold water. Bring to a boil over high heat. Reduce heat to medium; cook about 15 minutes or until potatoes are tender. Drain; return to pan. Mash with fork or potato masher. Meanwhile, melt butter in small skillet until sizzling. Add garlic; cook over medium-high, about 2 minutes or until garlic is golden brown. Add the cream; cook about 7 minutes or until cream has been reduced by half. Add garlic cream, salt and pepper to potatoes; mix well. Serve immediately.

Prepare the fish: steam the steelhead over moderate steam for 7 minutes. Drain off any excess liquid and combine the fish with the remaining steelhead ingredients. Shape the fish mixture into 7 or 8 patties. Melt 2 tablespoons butter in large skillet over medium heat until sizzling. Place 4 patties in skillet. Sauté, about 3 minutes on each side or until patties are firm to the touch and golden brown. Repeat with remaining patties in remaining 2 tablespoons butter.

To dine, present fish cakes on individual plates with mashed potatoes and a salad mixed with herb sprigs.

4 servings.

Serve pan-seared steelhead fillets
with a sauce made of raisins, pine nuts,
onions, vinegar and citrus zest.

Steelhead
with Sweet and Sour Onions

2 tablespoons olive oil
2 sweet onions, sliced
⅓ cup cider vinegar
½ cup raisins
¼ cup toasted pine nuts
2 teaspoons grated lemon peel
4 (8 ounce each) steelhead fillets
½ teaspoon salt
½ teaspoon coarse ground pepper
1 tablespoon fresh lemon juice

Heat 1 tablespoon olive oil in large skillet. Add onions; cook over medium heat about 6 minutes or until browned. Stir in vinegar, raisins, pine nuts and lemon peel. Remove from pan; set aside. In same skillet; add remaining 1 tablespoon olive oil. Place fillets in pan; season with salt and pepper. Cook over medium-high heat about 4 minutes on each side. Splash with lemon juice. Add onion mixture to pan. Continue cooking, stirring occasionally, for 4 to 5 minutes or until fish fillets flake with fork.

6 servings.

Trout

The Dynamic Trout

For the cook...

Whether brook, brown, rainbow or laker, fresh coldwater trout are delicate and hesitant feeders yet powerful, forceful creatures that have delighted the palate since long before the hook was invented. Trout are "dynamic" because they're smart and hard-to-catch, but taste great as well (dynamic on the plate). On occasion, if you decide to keep one, most anglers have visions of the fire, the blackened skillet and delicately-browned trout sautéing in butter. As a stream-side delicacy, trout is famous.

For the angler...

Trout live in cold streams and lakes across most of North America. The sport of trout fishing has been romanticized in movies, books and revelations from one angler to another. As Mr. Aughenbaugh's story relates, trout fishing fulfills one of the less tangible outcomes all fisherman seek whether consciously or not.

For all of us...

In fishing we seek removal from the familiar, frantic lifestyles of our own species. A spot hidden from humans unburdens the spirit, releasing it to a realm of care-free, joyful calm. In the perpetual motion of the natural world we find peace. Trout bring us to such spots.

Sometimes the best things in life are next door, and we travel past them a hundred times in the quest for the best "fishing hole." I have such a stream ten minutes from my home.

Once at a beautiful hole containing a log jam, I tossed in my Mepps spinner and landed it on a log. I slowly dragged it off and watched it flutter into the shadows. Snap! The slack left my line and it grew taut. I quickly jerked the rod, setting the hook, thus beginning a dogfight that lasted a full five minutes or so it felt. I was totally speechless as I picked up, with shaking hands, a 4 lb., 25-inch brown trout. Catching a fish of this strength and size on 4 lb. test line in a stream you can almost jump across, it has to be experienced to be understood. "I had lassooed an elephant with a string in a city park" was my friends analogy.

Only once in my trips back to "the run" have I met up with another fisherman. All other times, footprints are the only evidence that someone else was there before me. I do not fish "the run" often. I hold it as a special reservation for when my soul needs a quick fix of big trout in small water in a valley untouched by the progress of man. No traffic, no noise, no trash or stress, just me in a stream dancing with trout. "The run" is too special to visit often.

Andrew Aughenbaugh
City and State withheld

Purée parsnips, garlic and herbs
then spoon into an herb-crusted trout for a comforting winter meal.

Trout Stuffed
with Root Vegetable Purée

VEGETABLE PURÉE
8 roasted parsnips
2 tablespoons butter
¼ cup chopped fresh Italian parsley
2 cloves garlic, coarsely chopped
¼ teaspoon salt

TROUT
4 trout (about 10-12 ounces each), cleaned with head and tail left on
¼ cup mixture of chopped fresh Italian parsley, thyme and sage leaves
¼ teaspoon salt
¼ teaspoon coarse ground pepper
2 tablespoons butter

Place all vegetable purée ingredients in blender container and purée. Stuff each of the 4 trout equally with the purée. Place 2 trout in large skillet; season with half of herb mixture, salt and pepper. Sauté in 1 tablespoon butter over medium heat, 5 minutes on each side, or until fish flakes with fork. Repeat with remaining trout.

To sauté, tie fish with kitchen string to enclose cavity and hold purée. A small amount of purée can be used for the stuffing; additional purée can be served with the fish.

4 servings.

*Stuff the cavity of your trout with this wild-morel mixture.
Springtime heaven!*

Trout Stuffed with Wild Mushrooms

WILD MUSHROOMS
1 pound fresh morel (or other) mushrooms
¼ cup butter
1 sweet onion, chopped
1 tablespoon chopped fresh rosemary leaves
1 tablespoon chopped fresh thyme leaves
½ teaspoon salt
½ teaspoon coarse ground pepper

TROUT
4 trout (about 10-12 ounces each), cleaned with head and tail left on
½ teaspoon salt
½ teaspoon coarse ground pepper
2 tablespoons butter

Place all wild mushroom ingredients in skillet. Sauté over medium-high heat for 10 to 12 minutes, until mushrooms are browned and tender. Stuff each of the 4 trout equally with the sautéed mushrooms. Place 2 trout in large skillet; season with ¼ teaspoon salt and pepper. Sauté in 1 tablespoon butter over medium heat, 5 minutes on each side, or until fish flakes with fork. Repeat with remaining trout.

To sauté, tie fish with kitchen string to enclose cavity and hold mushrooms. A small amount of mushrooms can be used for the stuffing; additional mushrooms can be served over the sautéed fish.

4 servings.

Make a wild rice relish with autumn apples, herbs and onions,
then stuff inside pan-fried trout.

Wild Rice Relish and Trout

WILD RICE

2 tablespoons butter
2 cups cooked long grain wild rice
1 tart apple, chopped
1 sweet onion, chopped
2 cloves garlic, coarsely chopped
1 tablespoon chopped fresh thyme leaves
1 teaspoon salt
1 teaspoon coarse ground pepper

TROUT

4 trout (about 10-12 ounces each), cleaned with head and tail left on
2 tablespoons butter
2 cloves garlic, coarsely chopped
1 teaspoon chopped fresh thyme leaves
½ teaspoon coarse ground pepper

Place all wild rice ingredients in skillet. Sauté over medium heat, stirring occasionally, about 10 minutes or until apple and onion are tender. Stuff each of the 4 trout equally with the wild rice. Place 2 trout in large skillet; season with half of garlic, thyme and pepper. Sauté in 1 tablespoon butter over medium heat, 5 minutes on each side, or until fish flakes with fork. Repeat with remaining trout.

To sauté, tie fish with kitchen string to enclose cavity and hold the rice. The additional rice can be served over the sautéed fish.

4 servings.

*Roast summertime corn on the cob, remove kernels from the ear
and stuff inside the trout with cilantro and tomatoes.*

Roasted Corn-Stuffed Trout

ROASTED CORN
2 cups fresh corn kernels
2 tablespoons olive oil
½ cup sliced green onions
2 tablespoons chopped fresh cilantro
2 cloves garlic, coarsely chopped
1 ripe tomato, chopped
½ teaspoon salt
½ teaspoon coarse ground pepper

TROUT
4 trout (about 10-12 ounces each), cleaned with head and tail left on
1 tablespoon Dijon-style mustard
½ teaspoon salt
½ teaspoon coarse ground pepper
2 tablespoons butter

Place corn in skillet with 1 tablespoon olive oil. Roast over medium heat, stirring occasionally, about 6 minutes or until tender. Add remaining 1 tablespoon olive oil, onions, cilantro and garlic. Continue to sauté for 4 to 5 minutes or until vegetables are roasted. Stir in tomato, salt and pepper. Stuff each of the 4 trout equally with the roasted corn. Place 2 trout in large skillet; season with half of mustard, salt and pepper. Sauté in 1 tablespoon butter over medium heat, 5 minutes on each side, or until fish flakes with fork. Repeat with remaining trout.

To sauté, tie fish with kitchen string to enclose cavity and hold corn. Corn mixture can be doubled so extra corn can be served along side of fish.

4 servings.

Wrap trout in bacon and cook over an open fire. Serve with corncakes.

Breakfast Pan-Fried Brook Trout

CORN CAKES
3 large eggs
2 ½ cups fresh corn kernels
½ cup sliced green onions
½ cup stone ground cornmeal
1 teaspoon salt
½ teaspoon pepper
3 large egg whites
2 teaspoons olive oil

TROUT
8 freshly caught brook trout
¼ cup flour
¼ cup stone ground cornmeal
1 teaspoon dried thyme leaves
¼ teaspoon salt
8 slices bacon

Prepare grill or wood fire: heat until coals are ash white or a wood fire has burned down to coals.

Make the corn cakes: place 3 eggs and 1 ½ cups corn in blender or food processor fitted with a steel blade; mix until smooth. Pour into mixing bowl; add onions, cornmeal, salt, pepper and remaining 1 cup corn. Whip 3 egg whites in stainless steel bowl until they hold their peaks. Fold into the corn mixture. Place large skillet over medium coals; add oil. Drop quarter-cupfuls of the pancake batter, a few at a time, into the hot skillet. Cook pancakes, about 2 minutes per side. Place pancakes on a baking sheet as they are finished.

Prepare the fish: clean, wash and pat fish dry. Combine flour, cornmeal, thyme and salt. Roll fish in cornmeal mixture; tap off excess. Wrap each trout with bacon; secure with wooden pick. Place 4 fish in large skillet. Fry fish over medium-hot coals, about 5 minutes on each side. Fry until fish is firm to the touch and golden brown.

To dine, present trout with corn cakes and maple syrup.

6 servings.

Bake dressed trout with thin slices of sweet potatoes
and wedges of mildly-spiced Anaheim chile peppers.

Baked Trout
with Chile Seasoned Sweet Potatoes

SWEET POTATOES
3 medium (about 2-inch diameter) sweet potatoes, sliced into ½-inch rounds
2 Anaheim chile peppers, seeded, cut into thin wedges
1 teaspoon grated orange peel
2 tablespoons fresh orange juice
1 tablespoon olive oil
½ teaspoon salt
½ teaspoon coarse ground pepper

TROUT
4 trout (about 8-10 ounces each), cleaned with head removed
1 tablespoon olive oil
¼ cup chopped fresh parsley
2 teaspoons chili powder

Heat oven to 375°F. Place sweet potatoes and chile peppers in 13 x 9-inch baking pan; sprinkle with remaining sweet potato ingredients. Bake, stirring every 15 minutes, for 35 to 40 minutes or until potatoes are tender. Place trout on baked sweet potatoes; sprinkle with oil, parsley and chile powder. Continue baking for 10 to 12 minutes or until fish flakes with fork.

4 servings.

Toasted pumpkin seeds and the spices of cumin and chili powder
make a crust for pan-fried trout.

Pumpkin Seed Coated Trout

1 cup toasted pumpkin seeds, finely chopped
½ cup stone ground cornmeal
2 teaspoons chili powder
1 teaspoon ground cumin
½ teaspoon salt
½ teaspoon coarse ground pepper
4 trout (about 10-12 ounces each), cleaned with head and tail left on
1 egg, slightly beaten
¼ cup butter

Combine pumpkin seeds, cornmeal, chili powder, cumin, salt and pepper. Dip trout in egg; coat with pumpkin seed mixture. Heat 2 tablespoons butter in large skillet until sizzling. Place 2 trout in skillet. Sauté over medium-high heat about 5 minutes on each side. Remove from pan; keep warm. Repeat with remaining trout.

4 servings.

Sauté fillets of trout with zest of lemon and capers.

Lemon Trout Fillets
with Capers

2 tablespoons olive oil
2 anchovies, finely chopped
2 cloves garlic, coarsely chopped
1 tablespoon capers, crushed
2 teaspoons grated lemon peel
½ teaspoon coarse salt
½ teaspoon coarse ground pepper
4 trout fillets (about 8 ounces each)
2 tablespoons torn fresh basil leaves

Heat olive oil in large skillet; add anchovies, capers, lemon, salt and pepper. Cook over medium heat, stirring occasionally, about 2 minutes or until capers and garlic begin to brown. Place trout fillets in skillet. Sauté about 3 minutes on each side or until fish flakes with fork. Stir in torn basil leaves.

4 servings.

Season the trout with fresh-grated horseradish, coarse pepper and salt.

Horseradish Spiced Trout

2 tablespoons butter, softened
2 tablespoons chopped fresh rosemary
½ teaspoon coarse ground pepper
½ teaspoon coarse salt
2 tablespoons grated fresh horseradish
4 trout (about 10-12 ounces each), cleaned with head and tail left on

Prepare grill or wood fire: heat until coals are ash white or a wood fire has burned down to coals. Stir together all ingredients except trout. Place about 1 teaspoon butter mixture in cavity of each trout. Place trout on oiled grate of grill. Brush with softened butter. Grill over medium-hot coals about 5 minutes. Turn fish; brush with remaining butter. Grill about 5 minutes or until fish flakes with fork.

4 servings.

The Elusive Walleye

For the cook...

Fresh walleye with its snowy white, fine-flaked, sweet and tender properties may be the ultimate freshwater eating fish. The walleye is often filleted, and walleye fillets sautéed over a campfire on a wild shore are seldom forgotten. Walleye can be grilled, pan-fried, baked or broiled. Don't forget—sauger are closely related, and equally wonderful on the table.

For the angler...

The walleye is a strong, determined fighter. Though walleye is sometimes referred to as walleyed pike, it is not like pike at all but a member of the perch family, closely related to the sweet yellow perch. Fishing for walleye, as Mr. Ferland's story shows us, brings out the essentially romantic nature most of us harbor deep within.

For us all...

Fishing, after all, is a courtship between the angler and the fish. Resourceful, we tirelessly plot new strategies to captivate the beloved...in this case, the elusive walleye. We study its habits and place ourselves in its path. Armed with baits both alive and artificial, we keep this vigil by the light of day and by the moon's gentle glow, forever hopeful to lure a wall-eyed, golden-flanked fighter.

I have a home about 200 ft. from the shores of the magnificent St. Lawrence River, where the Lachine white water rapids end. One autumn evening, I went back to my favorite northern pike spot with a small "Daredevil" (red and white spoon).

By 9:45 p.m., under a bright full moon, I was still trying for my first real catch of the evening after netting two very small northerns. I was at the point where every cast was going to be the last one when I got a heavy strike. A loud splash of a tail led me to believe I had finally found a fair-sized northern, but the fighting pattern was not consistent with that variety of freshwater predator.

It took me the better part of a half hour to finally get my catch to shore from the violent currents of the mighty St. Lawrence. That's when I saw it...a BIG walleye.

I don't fish for competition, so I didn't weigh him. My 78-year-old fisherman/landlord, who was good enough to snap a photo for me, estimated my catch at 10 lbs. So it's true! As others have speculated, walleyes do bite in the fall and under bright moonlight!

Pierre Ferland
Schaumburg, IL

A summer dish bakes the fillets with ripe tomatoes and basil.

Basil and Tomato
Grilled Walleye

2 tablespoons herb flavored olive oil
4 (about 6-8 ounces each) walleye fillets
2 ripe tomatoes, sliced
½ cup basil leaves
2 cloves garlic, coarsely chopped
1 teaspoon coarse salt
1 teaspoon coarse ground pepper

Prepare grill or wood fire: heat until coals are ash white or a wood fire has burned down to coals. Cut four 1-foot-square sheets of aluminum foil. Drizzle each sheet with oil; on each sheet place 1 walleye fillet. Divide tomato slices, basil, garlic, salt and pepper equally over each portion. Fold the aluminum foil to cover the fish. Place over hot coals; grill for 10 to 12 minutes.

4 servings.

Winter finds a blend of pears and tart cranberries accompanying the walleye.

Cranberry and Pear Glazed Walleye

2 tablespoons butter
4 (about 6-8 ounces each) walleye fillets
2 ripe pears, sliced into thin wedges
½ cup fresh or frozen cranberries
2 tablespoons sugar
1 teaspoon dried thyme leaves
½ teaspoon salt
½ teaspoon pepper

Prepare grill or wood fire: heat until coals are ash white or a wood fire has burned down to coals. Cut four 1-foot-square sheets of aluminum foil. Rub each sheet with butter; on each sheet place 1 walleye fillet. Divide pears, cranberries, sugar, thyme, salt and pepper equally over each portion. Fold the aluminum foil to cover the fish. Place over hot coals; grill for 10 to 12 minutes.

4 servings.

Walleye fillets baked in foil with spring asparagus and zest of lemon.

Grilled Walleye
with Asparagus

2 tablespoons butter
4 (about 6-8 ounces each) walleye fillets
12 asparagus spears, broken into thirds
1 medium sweet onion, thinly sliced
1 lemon, cut into 8 thin slices
¼ cup snipped fresh chives
1 teaspoon salt
1 teaspoon coarse ground pepper

Prepare grill or wood fire: heat until coals are ash white or a wood fire has burned down to coals. Cut four 1-foot-square sheets of aluminum foil. Rub each sheet with butter; on each sheet place 1 walleye fillet, 3 asparagus spears, 2 onion slices, and 2 lemon slices. Sprinkle chives, salt and pepper equally over each portion. Fold the aluminum foil to cover the fish. Place over hot coals; grill for 10 to 12 minutes.

4 servings.

In autumn, add apples, onions and pecans
to flavor your walleye with the harvests of the season.

Toasted Pecan
and Apple Walleye

2 tablespoons butter
4 (about 6-8 ounces each) walleye fillets
2 tart apples, sliced into thin wedges
1 sweet onion, thinly sliced
½ cup chopped pecans, toasted
2 tablespoons pure maple syrup
½ teaspoon salt
½ teaspoon pepper

Prepare grill or wood fire: heat until coals are ash white or a wood fire has burned down to coals. Cut four 1-foot-square sheets of aluminum foil. Rub each sheet with butter; on each sheet place 1 walleye fillet. Divide apples, onion, pecans, syrup, salt and pepper equally over each portion. Fold the aluminum foil to cover the fish. Place over hot coals; grill for 10 to 12 minutes.

4 servings.

Broil whole walleye with sweet onion, red onion and shallots.

Walleye with Three-Onion Relish

WALLEYE
6 (¾ to 1 pound each) walleye, cleaned
2 tablespoons dried parsley flakes
½ teaspoon salt
¼ teaspoon pepper
1 tablespoon country-style Dijon mustard
1 tablespoon balsamic vinegar

RELISH
1 red onion, coarsely chopped
1 sweet onion, coarsely chopped
1 cup sliced shallots, leeks or other onions
1 teaspoon mustard seed
¼ teaspoon salt
¼ teaspoon pepper
2 tablespoons balsamic vinegar
1 tablespoon olive oil

Prepare the fish: clean, wash and pat fish dry. Combine remaining ingredients. Brush fish with herb mixture. Heat broiler; place fish on greased broiler pan. Broil fish 6 to 8 inches from heat, turning after 5 minutes. Brush with herb mixture; broil about 5 minutes or until fish flakes with fork.

Make the relish: stir together all relish ingredients in skillet. Cook over medium heat until onions are tender (8 to 10 minutes). Serve warm or at room temperature with fish.

6 servings.

Coat green tomatoes and walleye
with a cornmeal mixture. Then pan fry.

Walleye with Fried Green Tomatoes

1 cup flour
1 cup polenta-style cornmeal
2 teaspoons fresh thyme leaves
2 teaspoons grated lemon peel
½ teaspoon salt
½ teaspoon pepper
¼ teaspoon cayenne pepper
2 eggs, slightly beaten
3 medium green tomatoes
8 (about 5-6 ounces each) walleye fillets
¼ cup vegetable oil

Prepare grill or wood fire: heat until coals are ash white or a wood fire has burned down to coals.

Combine flour, cornmeal, thyme, lemon peel, salt, pepper and cayenne. Dip green tomato slices and walleye in egg; coat with flour mixture. Heat oil in a large skillet over wood fire or over medium-high heat. Fry tomatoes, 1 minute on each side. Remove from pan; keep warm. (If the oil begins to burn, wipe out the pan and add new oil.) Fry fish, about 2 minutes on each side. Fry until fish flakes with fork.

To dine, present tomatoes on plate with field greens. Top with walleye.

4 servings.

Top a corn tortilla with a mixture of chilled pico de gallo and walleye salad.

Walleye Tostada

PICO DE GALLO
2 ripe tomatoes, chopped
1 medium red onion, chopped
3 serrano or jalapeño chiles, seeded and minced
2 cloves garlic, minced
¼ cup coarsely chopped fresh cilantro
2 tablespoons fresh lime juice
½ teaspoon salt
½ teaspoon coarse ground pepper

WALLEYE
4 (about 6-8 ounces each) walleye fillets
1 tablespoon olive oil
1 teaspoon grated lime peel
½ teaspoon cumin powder
¼ teaspoon coarse ground pepper
8 corn tortillas

Make the pico de gallo: combine all ingredients in small bowl; let stand 1 hour. Transfer to glass jar; this sauce can be refrigerated up to 10 days.

Prepare grill or wood fire: heat until coals are ash white or a wood fire has burned down to coals.

Prepare the fish: brush fillets with olive oil; sprinkle with lime, cumin and pepper. Place on grill. Grill over hot coals, 4 minutes on each side or until fish flakes with fork. Place corn tortillas on grill. Grill, 2 minutes on each side or until tortillas are crispy.

To dine, present fish on tortillas with pico de gallo.

4 servings.

Enjoy grilled new potatoes and walleye with garlic, rosemary and coarse salt and pepper.

Rosemary Potatoes
and Walleye Fillets

3 tablespoons olive oil

16 small red potatoes

1 teaspoon coarse salt

1 teaspoon coarse ground pepper

4 (about 6-8 ounces each) walleye fillets

1 tablespoon chopped fresh rosemary leaves

2 cloves garlic, coarsely chopped

Prepare grill or wood fire: heat until coals are ash white or a wood fire has burned down to coals. Heat oil in a large skillet. Fry potatoes seasoned with salt and pepper, about 10 minutes or until almost tender. Place fillets around potatoes; season with rosemary and garlic. Fry fish, about 4 minutes on each side or until fish flakes with fork.

4 servings.

Serve new potatoes, green beans and hard-cooked eggs
in a mixed-green salad with broiled or grilled walleye.

Walleye Herbed Potato Salad

SALAD
2 pounds small red potatoes, quartered
½ pound fresh green beans
1 cup chopped fresh basil leaves
½ cup thinly sliced green onions
¼ cup white wine vinegar
1 tablespoon olive oil
2 teaspoons Dijon mustard
½ teaspoon salt
½ teaspoon coarse ground pepper
6 cloves garlic, coarsely chopped
3 ripe tomatoes, chopped

WALLEYE
4 (about 6-8 ounces each) walleye fillets
1 tablespoon olive oil
2 hard cooked eggs
2 cups mixed salad greens

Make the salad: place potatoes in a Dutch oven; cover with water. Bring to a boil; cook 10 minutes. Add beans and cook 6 minutes or until tender. Drain. Combine all remaining salad ingredients except tomatoes. Add potatoes, beans and tomatoes. Cover and chill. This salad can be refrigerated for up to 3 days.

Prepare the fish: heat broiler; place fish on greased broiler pan. Broil fish 6 to 8 inches from heat, turning after 3 minutes. Brush with olive oil; broil about 3 minutes or until fish flakes with fork. Flake fish into pieces; add to salad.

To dine, present salad on bed of salad greens, top with sliced hard cooked eggs.

6 servings.

A perfect recipe for walleye from the deep, cool, pine-lined lakes of the North.

Marinated Artichokes
and Walleye Fillets

4 (about 6-8 ounces each) walleye fillets
6 ounce jar marinated artichokes, reserve marinade
2 cloves garlic, coarsely chopped
2 tablespoons chopped fresh parsley
1 tablespoon grated orange peel
1 tablespoon fresh orange juice

Place fillets in skillet with 2 tablespoons reserved marinade. Sauté fish over medium-high heat, about 3 minutes on each side. Add remaining ingredients around fillets. Sauté until artichokes are heated through and fish flakes with fork.

4 servings.

A cold soup made with tomatoes, cucumber, red pepper and sautéed walleye.

Walleye Gazpacho

SOUP
¼ pound crustless French or Italian bread, torn into coarse chunks
4 ripe tomatoes, cut into pieces
1 sweet onion, chopped
2 cloves garlic
1 cucumber, peeled, seeded and cut into chunks
1 red pepper, cut into chunks
2 tablespoons olive oil
¼ cup red wine vinegar
½ teaspoon salt
½ teaspoon coarse ground pepper

WALLEYE
4 (about 6-8 ounces each) walleye fillets
1 tablespoon olive oil
¼ teaspoon cayenne pepper
2 teaspoons grated lemon peel
2 teaspoons chopped fresh dill weed

Make the soup: pour water over bread to cover, then squeeze out the water and place bread in bowl of food processor. Place remaining soup ingredients in food processor. Puree for 2 minutes or until smooth. Cover and chill. This soup can be refrigerated for up to 3 days.

Prepare the fish: sauté fish in skillet over medium-high heat in olive oil. Season with cayenne and lemon peel. Sauté until fish flakes with fork. Flake fish into pieces; add to soup. Sprinkle with dill weed.

To dine, add chopped cucumber, tomato and sprig of dill.

4 servings.

Half-pound, whole walleye are cornmeal-crusted and pan-fried.

Cornmeal Shore Lunch

6 (¾-1 pound each) walleye, cleaned
½ cup cornmeal
¼ cup flour
1 teaspoon salt
1 teaspoon dried basil leaves
½ teaspoon pepper
¼ teaspoon cayenne pepper
3 tablespoons butter
3 tablespoons olive oil

Prepare a wood fire: heat until fire has burned down to coals.

Prepare the fish: clean, wash and pat fish dry. Combine cornmeal, flour, salt, basil, pepper and cayenne. Roll fish in cornmeal mixture; tap off excess. Heat butter and oil in a skillet large enough to hold at least one fish. Fry fish, about 7 minutes on each side. Fry until fish is firm to the touch and golden brown.

6 servings.

Honey, mustard and vinegar combine to make a sauce
you can brush on walleye while grilling the fillets
with sweet onions and mushrooms.

Mustard Barbecued Walleye

BARBECUE SAUCE
¾ cup honey
½ cup yellow mustard
¼ cup white vinegar
½ teaspoon coarse salt
½ teaspoon coarse ground pepper

WALLEYE
6 (about 6-8 ounces each) walleye fillets
2 sweet onions, thickly sliced
¾ pound whole mushrooms

Make the sauce: combine all sauce ingredients in medium saucepan; cook over medium heat, stirring occasionally, until slightly thickened, about 5 minutes. Cool completely, transfer to jar. This sauce can be refrigerated up to a month.

Prepare grill or wood fire: heat until coals are ash white or a wood fire has burned down to coals.

Prepare the fish: brush fillets, onions and mushrooms with barbecue sauce; place on grill. Grill over medium-hot coals, basting occasionally, 4 minutes on each side or until fish flakes with fork and vegetables are tender.

6 servings.

Fish and Its Crusts

To use the crust mixtures, just dip the fish in egg,

buttermilk or beer. Coat the fish with the crumb

mixture. Brush the fish with olive oil or butter and

sprinkle with the herb or nut crusts.

The final touch for all of these crusts is a few

shakes of fresh ground pepper.

This group of recipes offers wonderful mixtures to make a variety of crusts for fish. Use these mixtures as the breading for baked, broiled, pan-fried and fried fish. As for ingredients, you'll find herbs, nuts, grated cheeses, bread crumbs, wheat and rye. Cracker coatings, cornmeal and flour mixtures also provide interesting textures and seasonings to the fish. These mixtures complement most any freshwater fish discussed in this cookbook.

You'll also enjoy the grated cheese blends offered here. They are designed to be sprinkled on fish during the last few minutes of baking, broiling or pan-frying.

The cheese blends need to be kept in the refrigerator or cooler. The bread crumbs stay fresh in the freezer. Simply dry out the crumbs before using by spreading them out on a cookie sheet. The other mixtures are staples and can be made ahead and packed with the tackle. Be sure to date the crust mixtures since spices loose flavor after 6 months. We recommend that you buy herbs in small quantities so that they maintain their special flavor.

Brush fish with olive oil and lightly dust with this dry rub.

Fennel Spiced Crust

1 teaspoon coarse salt
1 teaspoon coarse ground pepper
1 teaspoon dried thyme leaves
1 teaspoon crushed fennel seeds
½ teaspoon ground ginger
¼ teaspoon ground coriander
¼ teaspoon crushed red pepper flakes

Combine ingredients in a small bowl. Place in plastic bag or cannister.

Seasoning for 1 dozen fish.

Pumpkin, cilantro and cornmeal create a beautiful blend of harvest colors and flavors.

Pumpkin Crust

1 cup toasted pumpkin seeds, chopped
¼ cup stone ground cornmeal
¼ cup chili powder
½ cup chopped fresh cilantro leaves
1 teaspoon grated lemon peel
2 tablespoons olive oil

Combine ingredients in a small bowl. Place in plastic bag or cannister. Before using, blend olive oil into crust mixture. Rub onto fish fillets.

Seasoning for 1 dozen fish.

Fennel Spiced Crust

Dip fish fillets in fresh lemon juice and coat with coconut that is accented with ginger and mustard.

Gingered Mustard

¼ cup Dijon-style mustard
1 tablespoon finely grated ginger root
½ teaspoon coarse salt
½ teaspoon coarse ground pepper
¼ cup unsweetened coconut

Combine all ingredients except coconut in a small bowl. Place in tightly covered container. Refrigerate up to 1 month. Stir in coconut. Dip fish in lemon or lime juice; brush mustard on fish.

Seasoning for 1 dozen fish.

Brown butter in a skillet and add the fish.
A sprinkling of this walnut rosemary blend adds a truly pleasant taste.

Rosemary Walnut Blend

1 cup toasted walnuts, finely chopped
1 teaspoon chopped peeled fresh ginger
1 teaspoon grated lemon peel
2 teaspoons chopped fresh rosemary leaves

Combine ingredients in a small bowl. Place in plastic bag and freeze up to 1 month.

Seasoning for 1 dozen fish.

The sweetness of walnuts and the distinct flavor of cilantro combine with mint to accent fish deliciously.

Walnut Cilantro Crust

½ cup coarsely chopped walnuts
¼ cup flour
1 teaspoon sweet paprika
1 cup chopped fresh cilantro leaves
½ cup chopped fresh mint leaves
¼ cup olive oil
2 tablespoons fresh lemon juice

Combine walnuts, flour, paprika, cilantro and mint in a small bowl. Place in plastic bag and freeze up to 1 month. Pan-fry 1 dozen walnut cilantro crusted fish in olive oil; squeeze lemon juice over fish.

Coating for 1 dozen fish.

This blend of coriander, anise, lemon and garlic is a sweet crust blend.

Anise Spiced Crust

2 tablespoons coriander seeds, crushed
2 tablespoons anise seeds, crushed
1 tablespoon grated lemon peel
2 cloves garlic, minced
1 teaspoon coarse salt
1 teaspoon coarse ground pepper

Combine ingredients in a small bowl. Place in plastic bag or cannister. Brush fish with olive oil; rub with spice mixture.

Seasoning for 1 dozen fish.

Parmesan Peppered Spice

The subtle flavors of buttermilk for the dip, flour and
semolina for the coating, and Parmesan, salt and
pepper for the spice, is welcomed on freshwater fish.

Parmesan Peppered Spice

½ cup flour
½ cup semolina
½ cup finely grated Parmesan cheese
½ teaspoon coarse salt
½ teaspoon coarse ground pepper

Combine ingredients in a small bowl. Place in plastic bag and freeze up to 1
month.

Coating for 1 dozen fish.

Honey sweetens and caramelizes the sesame and herb crust for fish.

Sesame Honey

¼ cup honey
¼ cup finely chopped red onion
¼ cup snipped fresh chives
½ teaspoon salt
½ teaspoon coarse ground pepper
2 tablespoons sesame seeds

Combine all ingredients exept sesame seeds in a small bowl. Refrigerate up to 2
to 3 days. Coat fish in honey mixture; sprinkle with sesame seeds.

Seasoning for 1 dozen fish.

Relish, Salsa and Pesto

Beyond relish, salsa and pesto, this chapter contains a
variety of dressings for fish. These recipes can be made
ahead and packed along for condiments, camping staples
and simple savory seasonings for the angler-cook.

The right baste or sauce can give fish either a subtle sweetness, a real tang or pack a spicy punch. Oil marinades and pesto add moisture to fish, keep it from sticking to the grill, and give fish a crisp and flavorful skin. Paste marinades give fish a savory crust and flavor. Seasonings and bastes give fish a burst of flavor on the outside, while salsas, sauces and relishes are served as complements to the fish after it is cooked. Sauces and relishes should have assertive character, to balance the smoky, rich taste of the grilled fish. Sauces with sugar or honey burn easily; put them on toward the end of cooking, or use with a low fire and a covered grill.

The tart, slightly salty flavor
of capers goes well with grilled fish.

Caper Italian Dressing

½ cup olive oil
2 tablespoons white wine vinegar
1 teaspoon Dijon-style mustard
½ teaspoon coarse ground pepper
¼ teaspoon salt
2 tablespoons capers, drained and slightly crushed
1 tablespoon finely chopped fresh basil leaves
2 teaspoons grated lemon peel

Whisk together the oil, vinegar, mustard, pepper and salt in small bowl. Add
remaining ingredients. Store in cool place for 1 to 2 days.

¾ cup.

Roasted red peppers blend with basil, garlic and Parmesan cheese.
This pesto can be used as a baste or rub for fish, and a stuffing.

Roasted Pepper Pesto

2 red peppers
1 cup basil leaves
¼ cup pinenuts
8 cloves garlic, coarsely chopped
½ cup olive oil
1 cup grated fresh Parmesan cheese

Prepare grill or wood fire: heat until coals are ash white or a wood fire has
burned down to coals. Place peppers on grill. Roast peppers over hot coals about
2 inches from heat, turning often, about 10 minutes or until all edges are
charred. Transfer peppers to a deep bowl or container; cover with plastic wrap.
Let stand until cool enough to handle. Rinse in cold water; peel off charred skin,
and remove seeds. Use immediately or refrigerate up to 1 week. Combine roasted peppers, basil, pinenuts, garlic and olive oil in food processor or blender
container. Purée about 3 minutes. Add enough additional olive oil to make a
fluid but not runny consistency. Stir in Parmesan cheese. Pesto can be frozen for
up to 1 month. Freeze small amounts in ice cube trays. Sauté 4 fish fillets in 1
cube of pesto. Season with additional cube of pesto.

2 cups.

Paste marinades are a combination
of dry ingredients moistened
with just enough oil or other
wet ingredients to bind them.
The seasonings are ground in a mortar,
minced fine or pulverized in a food processor,
after which oil is added just until the mixture
is moist enough to stick to the fish.

Peanut, Ginger and Lime Paste

½ cup salted roasted peanuts, minced
1 tablespoon minced fresh ginger root
1 tablespoon grated lime peel
2 cloves garlic, minced to a paste
1 tablespoon chopped fresh cilantro
¼ teaspoon salt
¼ teaspoon coarse ground pepper
Olive oil

Mix all the ingredients except the oil together in a small bowl. Add enough oil so that the dry ingredients are moist and the mixture forms a paste. Use immediately or let stand at room temperature for 2 to 3 days. Paste marinades are best on foods cooked over a medium-hot or low fire.

½ cup.

Brush this chutney over fish the last few minutes of grilling,
or serve as a sauce for fish. This fruited sauce can also be used
as a dressing for salads and spread for bread.

Garlic Nectarine Chutney

4 medium ripe nectarines, cut into ½-inch pieces
1 ½ cups water
½ cup cider vinegar
½ cup sugar
2 tablespoons coarsely chopped fresh ginger root

Combine all ingredients in medium saucepan. Cook over medium heat, stirring
occasionally, 30 to 40 minutes or until thickened. Cover and refrigerate. This
sauce can be refrigerated for 3 to 5 days.

4 cups.

A jalapeño spiced cabbage slaw that can be packed along on a fishing outing
and served with fish or on a grilled fish sandwich. Try making a tortilla sandwich with flour tortillas.

Cabbage Jalapeño Slaw

¾ cup cider vinegar
¼ cup water
2 tablespoons coarse ground mustard
1 tablespoon seeded, finely chopped jalapeño pepper
½ teaspoon salt
½ teaspoon coarse ground pepper
4 cups shredded red cabbage

Combine all ingredients except cabbage in small bowl. Place cabbage in large
bowl; pour over dressing. Cover and refrigerate. Slaw can be refrigerated for 2 to
3 days.

4 cups.

Make flavor-infused oils with aromatic herbs, spices, garlic, chiles or citrus peel. Let it stand for as little as an hour for just a hint of flavor, or up to several weeks for a stronger infusion. Use for marinades and bastes for grilling.

Chile Infused Oil

16 ounce bottle olive oil
2 jalapeño peppers
Fresh lemon peel
5 mixed peppercorns

Pour olive oil into large bowl; add seasonings. Let stand at room temperature for 2 to 3 weeks. Remove peppers, lemon and peppercorns. Pour back into bottle. Use oil in paste marinades or salad dressings, or they can be used alone as a light oil baste before grilling fish.

2 cups.

Cucumber relish subtly complements fish.
Serve this relish with a fish sandwich, or on top of pan-fried fillets.

Minted Cucumber Relish

2 medium cucumbers, thinly sliced
1 medium red onion, thinly sliced
¼ cup cider vinegar
1 tablespoon olive oil
2 tablespoons chopped fresh mint leaves
1 teaspoon grated fresh ginger root

Combine all ingredients in medium bowl. Cover and refrigerate. This relish can be refrigerated for 1 to 2 days.

3 cups.

Blend mayonnaise with horseradish, mustard, lemon and dill weed.
This makes a delicious spread for fish sandwiches, or a dip for crusted fish.

Horseradish Mayonnaise

1 cup mayonnaise
2 tablespoons grated fresh or prepared horseradish
2 tablespoons Dijon-style mustard
2 teaspoons grated lemon peel
2 tablespoons chopped fresh dill weed
1/4 teaspoon pepper

Combine all ingredients in a medium bowl. Cover; refrigerate up to 1 week.

1 cup.

Thick and chunky salsa, carrots and tomatoes are spiced with cilantro and lime.
This is a healthy and flavorful salsa for tortillas, beans and grilled fish.

Carrot Salsa

1 ½ cups thick and chunky salsa
½ cup chopped fresh cilantro
4 carrots, coarsely chopped
1 red onion, coarsely chopped
2 ripe tomatoes, coarsely chopped
1 jalapeño pepper, seeded, finely chopped
1 tablespoon lime juice

Combine all ingredients in a medium bowl. Cover; refrigerate overnight or until
serving time.

3 cups.

Index

A

Anise Spiced Crusts, 143
Antipasto
    Antipasto Sandwich, 80
    Catfish Antipasto, 43
Appetizers
    Catfish Antipasto, 43
    Pesto and Tomato Fish Bruschetta, 76
Apples
    Apple Sage Stuffed Northern Pike, 54
    Bass with Walnut Butter and Apples, 23
    Fish, Corn and Apple Chowder, 16
    Toasted Pecan and Apple Walleye, 126
    Wild Rice Relish and Trout, 111
Artichokes
    Catfish Antipasto, 43
    Marinated Artichokes and Walleye Fillets, 134
Asparagus
    Grilled Walleye with Asparagus, 125

B

Bacon
    Fish, Corn and Apple Chowder, 16
    Fish and Lentil Soup, 17
    Panfish with Lentils and Bacon, 63
Baked Pike in Sour Cream and Paprika, 55
Baked Trout with Chile Seasoned Sweet Potatoes, 114
Barbecued Crappie, 72
Basil, 8
    Basil and Tomato Grilled Walleye, 122
    Catfish with Tomato Basil Cream, 40
Bass, 14–29
    Bass with Walnut Butter and Apples, 23
    Bread and Tomato Salad, 21
    Campers' Fish Hash, 28
    Fish, Corn and Apple Chowder, 16
    Fish and Lentil Soup, 17
    Garlic Roasted Bass, 29
    Herb Crusted Bass, 24
    Lemon Sesame Bass, 24
    Potato, Onion and Fish Pie, 25
    Summertime Tomato and Fish Stew, 19
    Sweet Corn Salad, 26
    Tender Spring Pea and Fish Soup, 20
Batter-Fried Catfish, 45
Beans
    Catfish with Red Beans and Rice, 38
    Salmon with Cannellini Beans, 95
Blackened Catfish with Fried Spring Onions, 33

Blackened Catfish with Pecans, 32
Bluegill
    Panfish with Fruited Couscous, 68
    Sun-Dried Tomatoes with Spinach and Panfish, 60
Bread and Tomato Salad, 21
Breakfast Pan-Fried Brook Trout, 113
Bruschetta
    Pesto and Tomato Fish Bruschetta, 76

C

Cabbage Jalapeño Slaw, 151
Campers' Fish Hash, 28
Capers
    Caper Italian Dressing, 148
    Caramelized Lemons and Caper Salmon Steaks, 92
    Lemon Trout Fillets with Capers, 117
Caramelized Lemons and Caper Salmon Steaks, 92
Carrots
    Carrot Salsa, 155
    Fish and Lentil Soup, 17
    Garlic Roasted Bass, 29
    Panfish with Lentils and Bacon, 63
    Tender Spring Pea and Fish Soup, 20
Catfish, 30–47
    Batter-Fried Catfish, 45
    Blackened Catfish with Fried Spring Onions, 33
    Blackened Catfish with Pecans, 32
    Catfish Antipasto, 43
    Catfish Fajitas, 37
    Catfish Jambalaya, 47
    Catfish with Red Beans and Rice, 38
    Catfish with Tomato Basil Cream, 40
    Chile Blackened Catfish, 36
    Layered Spinach and Catfish Bake, 44
    Mustard Blackened Catfish, 35
    Pan-Fried Catfish with Lemon and Garlic, 41
Celery
    Catfish Jambalaya, 47
    Fish and Okra Gumbo, 46
Cheese
    Spinach and Feta Sautéed with Salmon Steaks, 90
Chile Peppers
    Baked Trout with Chile Seasoned Sweet Potatoes, 114
    Cabbage Jalapeño Slaw, 151
    Catfish Fajitas, 37
    Chile Blackened Catfish, 36
    Chile Infused Oil, 153
    Fish Cakes with Roasted Squash Purée, 103
    Roasted Peppers with Salmon, 85
    Seared Salmon Steaks with Minted Chutney, 93

Walleye Tostado, 130

Chowder. *See* Soups

Chutney
Garlic Nectarine Chutney, 151
Seared Salmon Steaks with Minted Chutney, 93

Cilantro
Walnut Cilantro Crust, 143

Citrus Marinated Salmon, 88

Corn
Breakfast Pan-Fried Brook Trout, 113
Chile Blackened Catfish, 36
Fish, Corn and Apple Chowder, 16
Panfish Creole, 72
Roasted Corn-Stuffed Trout, 112
Sweet Corn Salad, 26

Cornmeal Shore Lunch, 136

Corn Salsa, 36

Couscous
Panfish with Fruited Couscous, 68

Cranberries
Cranberry and Pear Glazed Walleye, 123
Fish with Glazed Cranberries, 52

Crappie
Barbecued Crappie, 72
Curried Eggs and Panfish, 62
Garlic Chip Crappie Sandwiches, 70
Panfish with Lentils and Bacon, 63
Pesto Crappie with Tomato Slices, 65
Sweet Potato Cakes Stacked with Panfish, 58

Crusts, 138–145
Anise Spiced Crusts, 143
Fennel Spiced Crusts, 140
Gingered Mustard, 141
Parmesan Peppered Spice, 145
Pumpkin Crust, 140
Rosemary Walnut Blend, 141
Sesame Honey, 145
Walnut Cilantro Crust, 143

Cucumbers
Bread and Tomato Salad, 21
Minted Cucumber Relish, 154
Open-Faced Fish Sandwich with Cucumber Slaw, 77
Poached Salmon with Cucumber Sauce, 89
Walleye Gazpacho, 135

Curried Eggs and Panfish, 62

D

Dried Fruits
Panfish with Fruited Couscous, 68

E

Eggs
Curried Eggs and Panfish, 62
Sun-Dried Tomatoes with Spinach and Panfish, 60

F

Fajitas
Catfish Fajitas, 37

Fennel
Fennel Spiced Crusts, 140
Salmon Kabobs with Fennel, 97
Summertime Tomato and Fish Stew, 19

Fish
checking for doneness, 11, 12
filleting, 13
freezing, 13
fresh, 12–13

Fish, Corn and Apple Chowder, 16

Fish and Lentil Soup, 17

Fish and Okra Gumbo, 46

Fish Cakes
Fish Cakes with Roasted Squash Purée, 103
Mustard Spiced Fish Cakes, 101
Pan-Seared Fish Cakes with Garlic Mashed Potatoes, 104
Tandoori Fish Cakes, 100

Fish with Glazed Cranberries, 52

G

Garlic, 8
Garlic Chip Crappie Sandwiches, 70
Garlic Nectarine Chutney, 151
Garlic Roasted Bass, 29
Pan-Fried Catfish with Lemon and Garlic, 41
Summertime Tomato and Fish Stew, 19

Ginger
Gingered Mustard, 141
Steamed Salmon with Scallions and Ginger, 96

Grapefruit
Sunfish with Red Onion and Citrus, 67

Green Beans
Walleye Herbed Potato Salad, 133

Grilled Panfish with Salsa Verde, 71

Grilled Salmon with Spring Herbs, 87

Grilled Walleye with Asparagus, 125

Grilling, 10–12

Gumbo. *See* Soups

H

Herb Crusted Bass, 24

Herbed Tomato Vinaigrette Salmon, 84

Honey
     Sesame Honey, 145
Horseradish
     Horseradish Mayonnaise, 155
     Horseradish Spiced Trout, 119

J
Jerk Seasoned Perch, 81

K
Kabobs
     Salmon Kabobs with Fennel, 97

L
Layered Spinach and Catfish Bake, 44
Lemons
     Caramelized Lemons and Caper Salmon Steaks, 92
     Lemon Sesame Bass, 24
     Lemon Trout Fillets with Capers, 117
     Pan-Fried Catfish with Lemon and Garlic, 41
Lentils
     Fish and Lentil Soup, 17
     Panfish with Lentils and Bacon, 63

M
Main Dish Pies
     Potato, Onion and Fish Pie, 25
Marinated Artichokes and Walleye Fillets, 134
Mushrooms
     Mustard Barbecued Walleye, 137
     Trout Stuffed with Wild Mushrooms, 109
Mustard
     Gingered Mustard, 141
     Mustard Barbecued Walleye, 137
     Mustard Blackened Catfish, 35
     Mustard Spiced Fish Cakes, 101

N
Nectarines
     Garlic Nectarine Chutney, 151
Nightshade family, 8–9
Northern Pike, 48–55
     Apple Sage Stuffed Northern Pike, 54
     Baked Pike in Sour Cream and Paprika, 55
     Fish with Glazed Cranberries, 52
     Onion Relish Stuffed Northern Pike, 51
     Savory Tomato Stuffed Pike, 50
Nuts
     Bass with Walnut Butter and Apples, 23
     Blackened Catfish with Pecans, 32
     Fish with Glazed Cranberries, 52

Peanut, Ginger and Lime Paste, 150
Rosemary Walnut Blend, 141
Toasted Pecan and Apple Walleye, 126
Walnut Cilantro Crust, 143

O
Okra
     Fish and Okra Gumbo, 46
Onions
     Baked Pike in Sour Cream and Paprika, 55
     Blackened Catfish with Fried Spring Onions, 33
     Bread and Tomato Salad, 21
     Catfish Antipasto, 43
     Catfish Fajitas, 37
     Catfish Jambalaya, 47
     Herbed Tomato Vinaigrette Salmon, 84
     Layered Spinach and Catfish Bake, 44
     Onion Relish Stuffed Northern Pike, 51
     Panfish Creole, 72
     Steelhead with Sweet and Sour Onions, 105
     Summertime Tomato and Fish Stew, 19
     Sunfish with Red Onions and Citrus, 67
     Sweet Corn Salad, 26
     Walleye with Three-Onion Relish, 127
Open-Faced Fish Sandwich with Cucumber Slaw, 77
Oranges
     Citrus Marinated Salmon, 88
     Salmon Kabobs with Fennel, 97

P
Panfish, 56–73
     Barbecued Crappie, 72
     Curried Eggs and Panfish, 62
     Grilled Panfish with Salsa Verde, 71
     Panfish Creole, 72
     Panfish with Fruited Couscous, 68
     Panfish with Lentils and Bacon, 63
     Pesto Crappie with Tomato Slices, 65
     Sun-Dried Tomatoes with Spinach and Panfish, 60
     Sunfish with Red Onions and Citrus, 67
     Sweet Potato Cakes Stacked with Panfish, 58
     Tuscan Grilled Panfish, 66
Pan-Fried Catfish with Lemon and Garlic, 41
Parmesan Cheese
     Herb Crusted Bass, 24
     Parmesan Peppered Spice, 145
Parsnips
     Trout Stuffed with Root Vegetable Puree, 108
Peaches
     Peach Fisherman's Sandwich, 78
Peanut, Ginger and Lime Paste, 150

Pears
    Cranberry and Pear Glazed Walleye, 123
Peas
    Tender Spring Pea and Fish Soup, 20
Pecans
    Blackened Catfish with Pecans, 32
    Toasted Pecan and Apple Walleye, 126
Peppers. *See also* Chile Peppers
    Campers' Fish Hash, 28
    Catfish Antipasto, 43
    Catfish Fajitas, 37
    Panfish Creole, 72
    Potato, Onion and Fish Pie, 25
    Roasted Pepper Pesto, 149
    Walleye Gazpacho, 135
Perch, 73–81
    Antipasto Sandwich, 80
    Jerk Seasoned Perch, 81
    Open-Faced Fish Sandwich with Cucumber Slaw, 77
    Peach Fisherman's Sandwich, 78
    Pesto and Tomato Fish Bruschetta, 76
Pesto and Tomato Fish Bruschetta, 76
Pesto Crappie with Tomato Slices, 65
Poached Salmon with Cucumber Sauce, 89
Potatoes, 9
    Campers' Fish Hash, 28
    Fish, Corn and Apple Chowder, 16
    Pan-Seared Fish Cakes with Garlic Mashed Potatoes, 104
    Potato, Onion and Fish Pie, 25
    Rosemary Potatoes and Walleye Fillets, 131
    Walleye Herbed Potato Salad, 133
Pumpkin
    Pumpkin Crust, 140
    Pumpkin Seed Coated Trout, 116

R

Relishes
    Minted Cucumber Relish, 154
Rice
    Catfish Jambalaya, 47
    Catfish with Red Beans and Rice, 38
    Wild Rice Relish and Trout, 111
Roasted Corn-Stuffed Trout, 112
Roasted Pepper Pesto, 149
Roasted Peppers with Salmon, 85
Rosemary Potatoes and Walleye Fillets, 131
Rosemary Walnut Blend, 141

S

Sage
    Apple Sage Stuffed Northern Pike, 54

Salads
    Bread and Tomato Salad, 21
    Cabbage Jalapeño Slaw, 151
    Sweet Corn Salad, 26
    Walleye Herbed Potato Salad, 133
Salmon, 82–97
    Caramelized Lemons and Caper Salmon Steaks, 92
    Citrus Marinated Salmon, 88
    Grilled Salmon with Spring Herbs, 87
    Herbed Tomato Vinaigrette Salmon, 84
    Poached Salmon with Cucumber Sauce, 89
    Roasted Peppers with Salmon, 85
    Salmon Kabobs with Fennel, 97
    Salmon with Cannellini Beans, 95
    Seared Salmon Steaks with Minted Chutney, 93
    Spinach and Feta Sautéed with Salmon Steaks, 90
    Steamed Salmon with Scallions and Ginger, 96
Sandwiches
    Antipasto Sandwich, 80
    Garlic Chip Crappie Sandwiches, 70
    Open-Faced Fish Sandwich with Cucumber Slaw, 77
    Peach Fisherman's Sandwich, 78
Sauces
    Caper Italian Dressing, 148
    Carrot Salsa, 155
    Chile Infused Oil, 153
    Corn Salsa, 36
    Garlic Nectarine Chutney, 151
    Horseradish Mayonnaise, 155
    Peanut, Ginger and Lime Paste, 150
Savory Tomato Stuffed Pike, 50
Scallions
    Steamed Salmon with Scallions and Ginger, 96
Seared Salmon Steaks with Minted Chutney, 93
Sesame Honey, 145
Soups. *See also* Stew
    Catfish Jambalaya, 47
    Fish, Corn and Apple Chowder, 16
    Fish and Lentil Soup, 17
    Fish and Okra Gumbo, 46
    Tender Spring Pea and Fish Soup, 20
    Walleye Gazpacho, 135
Spinach
    Blackened Catfish with Fried Spring Onions, 33
    Layered Spinach and Catfish Bake, 44
    Spinach and Feta Sautéed with Salmon Steaks, 90
    Sun-Dried Tomatoes with Spinach and Panfish, 60
Squash
    Catfish Antipasto, 43
    Fish Cakes with Roasted Squash Puree, 103
Steamed Salmon with Scallions and Ginger, 96

Steelhead, 98–105
    Fish Cakes with Roasted Squash Purée, 103
    Mustard Spiced Fish Cakes, 101
    Pan-Seared Fish Cakes with Garlic Mashed Potatoes, 104
    Steelhead with Sweet and Sour Onions, 105
    Tandoori Fish Cakes, 100
Stew. *See also* Soups
    Summertime Tomato and Fish Stew, 19
Sun-Dried Tomatoes with Spinach and Panfish, 60
Sunfish
    Grilled Panfish with Salsa Verde, 71
    Sunfish with Red Onions and Citrus, 67
Sweet Potatoes
    Baked Trout with Chile Seasoned Sweet Potatoes, 114
    Sweet Potato Cakes Stacked with Panfish, 58

T

Tacklebox spices, 8
Tandoori Fish Cakes, 100
Tender Spring Pea and Fish Soup, 20
Toasted Pecan and Apple Walleye, 126
Tomatillos
    Grilled Panfish with Salsa Verde, 71
Tomatoes, 8–9
    Basil and Tomato Grilled Walleye, 122
    Bread and Tomato Salad, 21
    Campers' Fish Hash, 28
    Carrot Salsa, 155
    Catfish Antipasto, 43
    Catfish Jambalaya, 47
    Catfish with Red Beans and Rice, 38
    Catfish with Tomato Basil Cream, 40
    Fish and Lentil Soup, 17
    Fish and Okra Gumbo, 46
    Garlic Chip Crappie Sandwiches, 70
    Herbed Tomato Vinaigrette Salmon, 84
    Panfish Creole, 72
    Panfish with Lentils and Bacon, 63
    Pesto and Tomato Fish Bruschetta, 76
    Pesto Crappie with Tomato Slices, 65
    Salmon with Cannellini Beans, 95
    Savory Tomato Stuffed Pike, 50
    Spinach and Feta Sautéed with Salmon Steaks, 90
    Summertime Tomato and Fish Stew, 19
    Sun-Dried Tomatoes with Spinach and Panfish, 60
    Sweet Corn Salad, 26
    Walleye Gazpacho, 135
    Walleye Herbed Potato Salad, 133
    Walleye Tostada, 130
    Walleye with Fried Green Tomatoes, 128

Tostadas
    Walleye Tostada, 130
Trout, 106–119
    Baked Trout with Chile Seasoned Sweet Potatoes, 114
    Breakfast Pan-Fried Brook Trout, 113
    Horseradish Spiced Trout, 119
    Lemon Trout Fillets with Capers, 117
    Pumpkin Seed Coated Trout, 116
    Roasted Corn-Stuffed Trout, 112
    Trout Stuffed with Root Vegetable Puree, 108
    Trout Stuffed with Wild Mushrooms, 109
    Wild Rice Relish and Trout, 111
Tuscan Grilled Panfish, 66

V

Vegetables, 9

W

Walleye, 120–137
    Basil and Tomato Grilled Walleye, 122
    Cornmeal Shore Lunch, 136
    Cranberry and Pear Glazed Walleye, 123
    Grilled Walleye with Asparagus, 125
    Marinated Artichokes and Walleye Fillets, 134
    Mustard Barbecued Walleye, 137
    Rosemary Potatoes and Walleye Fillets, 131
    Toasted Pecan and Apple Walleye, 126
    Walleye Gazpacho, 135
    Walleye Herbed Potato Salad, 133
    Walleye Tostada, 130
    Walleye with Fried Green Tomatoes, 128
    Walleye with Three-Onion Relish, 127
Walnuts
    Bass with Walnut Butter and Apples, 23
    Rosemary Walnut Blend, 141
    Walnut Cilantro Crust, 143
Watercress
    Onion Relish Stuffed Northern Pike, 51

Z

Zucchini
    Catfish Antipasto, 43
    Garlic Roasted Bass, 29